All About
Rifle Hunting
and Shooting
in America

All About Rifle Hunting and Shooting in America

Edited by Steve Ferber

Winchester Press

DEDICATION

To the memory of my parents, who encouraged my participation in the field of sports, this book is affectionately dedicated.

Picture Credits

Page 16: "Shooting for the Beef," by George Caleb Bingham, courtesy of The Brooklyn Museum, Dick S. Ramsey Fund. Page 17: "The Turkey Shoot," by Tompkins H. Matteson, courtesy of the New York State Historical Society. Page 22: Scene from "American Frontier Life," by Arthur Fitzwilliam Tate, courtesy of the Yale University Art Gallery, The Whitney Collection of Sporting Art.

Library of Congress Cataloging in Publication Data
Main entry under title:

All about rifle hunting and shooting in America.
  Includes index.
  1. Hunting—United States. 2. Shooting—United
States. 3. Rifles. I. Ferber, Steve.
SK38.A44   799.2'02832   77-22169
ISBN 0-87691-244-7

Published by Winchester Press
205 East 42nd Street
New York, N.Y. 10017

WINCHESTER is a Trademark of Olin Corporation used by Winchester Press, Inc. under authority and control of the Trademark Proprietor.

Printed in the United States of America

Contents

Rifle Talk

Part I

Good Rifles, Good Shots— An American Heritage

Robert Elman

Americans have always cherished marksmanship as a worthy skill. Traditionally, it has been a basis for pride. During the late 19th century, when good shooting was expected of any young man who grew up in rural America and helped to supply his family's table with meat, it was also a status symbol among city dwellers—proof that a man had the leisure time to master a gentlemanly art. But long before that, during the country's exploration, settlement, and expansion, it was a basis for something more than pride—survival. It both protected his life and got him his food.

Although the earliest firearms used in the New World were not rifled, the need for accurate shooting was of vital concern from the very dawn of discovery. On October 12, 1492, when Columbus set foot on the island he named San Salvador, his first landfall in the Western Hemisphere, he recorded in his journal that his landing party carried a "Turkish bow, a crossbow . . . and a hand gonne." The "hand gonne" was an *espingarda,* a triggerless matchlock shoulder arm, the immediate forerunner of the harquebuses used, together with cannons, during the next few decades to vanquish Indians. The principal advantage of the espingarda over earlier hand-cannons was that it could be aimed and fired more easily by a single soldier, without an assistant, and it was somewhat more accurate. The harquebus, which utilized a trigger, was still more conducive to aimed fire, and its trigger-activated ignition reduced the wavering inherent in the manual pivoting of the serpentine striker that held the lit match. In brief, it was a more accurate shoulder arm—a step closer to the efficiency that would ultimately be achieved when American settlers obtained their first rifles.

At Jamestown, the English colonists used muskets to harvest meat and deter Indian attacks. On the Hudson, the English and the rival Dutch of New Amsterdam occasionally trained their muskets and long fowlers on one another. At Plymouth and Massachusetts Bay, many of the Pilgrims armed themselves with long fowlers having 6½-foot, .75-caliber "musket bores" or 5½-foot, .69-caliber "bastard musket bores." Invariably those early fowling pieces were extremely long and heavy, but it was an era when accuracy and power were equated with a long bore. In 1621 Edward Winslow of Plymouth wrote home to prospective colonists advising them to "let your piece be long in the barrel and fear not the weight of it, for most of our shooting is from stands."

A year or so later, a Welsh family named Thomson (the spelling was modernized to "Thompson" by descendants) made the crossing to Plymouth. With them came their seven-year-old son John, who was to become a man of consequence in the Colony. One day in 1675, John Thomson admitted several aggressive natives—probably Wampanoags—to his cabin. According to family tradition, he sat calmly in a corner, holding his "long gun in his lap, having his brass pistol in his hand." The Indians left peaceably. But the Wampanoag chieftain—King Phillip, as the Colonists called him—was enraged by several instances of alleged English treachery. That spring, English obduracy and ineptitude in dealing with the natives sparked the brief but bloody War of King Philip. Thomson had charge of 16 men defending the little fort at Plymouth. He took great pride in his ability to aim his .84-caliber, 20½-pound, long fowler—*offhand*. But this time he handed the gun to Issac Howland, a noted marksman, with orders to shoot a warrior who stood on a boulder taunting the defenders from what he thought was a safe distance. The brave had sadly underestimated the range of English shoulder weapons, and the error cost him his life. The attack was repulsed. But even as early as 1675, the colonists were aware that better defense, as well as better hunting, could be facilitated by still more accurate arms, rifled arms.

Rifles were hardly a new invention. They were, however, expensive, scarce, and difficult to manufacture. The cutting of rifling grooves was an arduous, time-consuming process requiring a high degree of skill. The grooves had to be cut one at a time with a steel bit fastened to a long rod that was pulled through the bore. The rod was rotated at the desired rate, or pitch, by a stud that rode along a hand-cut spiral groove inside a long

wooden cylinder. This basic method and variations of it continued in use for several centuries—until well into the 20th, in fact —although the rifling itself was subjected to innumerable experiments to impart an ideal spin to a projectile and thus improve accuracy. The experiments included two-groove, polygonal, elliptical, and multigroove rifling, changes in pitch, deep and shallow grooving, and so on.

The development of rifling cannot be precisely dated, but it was used at the beginning of the 16th century and probably, at least in Germany or Austria, during the last half of the 15th. Had it been less costly and time-consuming to produce, surely it would have gained widespread popularity by the time the first waves of Pilgrims touched the shores of America. Indeed, it had already been used in Danish military arms, and by 1631 the Hessians were arming soldiers with rifles.

For military purposes, however, rifles had the disadvantage of being much slower and more difficult to load than smoothbores—despite early breechloading experiments conducted during the very period when rifling was being developed. For more than two centuries after the Danish and Hessian innovations, most soldiers were issued muskets, rifles being generally reserved for a few long-range, slow-firing sharpshooters. The first rifle to be manufactured in a United States government armory was the Harpers Ferry Model 1803.

A major breakthrough came in 1851, when Captain Claude E. Minié, a French army officer, introduced a hollow-based, cylindro-conoidal bullet that expanded as the propellant gas pushed it through a rifled bore. Since it expanded, it could be undersized, and could therefore be rammed down a rifled muzzle-loading barrel about as quickly as the traditional round ball and wad could be rammed home in a smoothbore. Several European nations immediately rifled their muskets to fire one version or another of the new "minie ball." And in 1855 the United States adopted two new shoulder arms and a pistol, all rifled for use

Early woodcut showing American field sports. In this first known picture of hunting in America, the ease of finding game is grossly exaggerated. The man in right foreground carries a musket, but would have preferred a longer fowling piece.

Gunsmithing establishment in the 16th century, when some craftsmen were already producing rifled arms as well as smoothbores.

Target match at Zurich in 1504. There is evidence that rifles were already being used in special events at such matches.

with the minie ball. One of the shoulder arms was a short rifle of the general type already used by hunters, target shooters, and a few military snipers. The other was a longer piece, the Model 1855 rifled musket, or rifle-musket as it came to be known. Percussion ignition had already made flintlocks obsolete, but the new rifled musket employed a system even newer than the standard percussion cap and nipple. It had a lock designed for the Maynard tape primer, invented by a Washington dentist named Edward Maynard. This provided automatic priming by individual charges of fulminate spaced along the tape—a device familiar to later generations of shooters whose first ''guns'' were toy cap pistols employing a roll of caps to produce a realistic noise with each pull of the trigger.

Unfortunately, the Maynard tape could tear, jam, fail to fire, or otherwise malfunction, and the Model 1861 rifled musket reverted to standard percussion operation. All the same, the introduction of the Model 1855 (and its direct descendants during the Civil War) proved the military value—the general value, in fact—of relatively fast-firing, reliable, accurate rifles.

French colonists in Florida, circa 1564, using matchlocks in battle with Indians.

Ironically, civilian marksmen had long known the value of rifles, even rifles that were admittedly slow to load. Firearms historians are fond of the old chestnut that improvements in civilian guns generally originate as military innovations, prompted by wartime needs. But quite often such developments have come about first in civilian arms, improved to satisfy the needs of hunters, and only later adopted by the military. So it was with rifles in America. In the early 1700's, German, Austrian, Dutch, and Swiss settlers had brought with them their *jaeger* rifles—literally, "hunter" rifles—and from these a uniquely American-type rifle gradually evolved.

Almost two centuries before that, central European marksmen had begun to use greased patches of cloth or thin leather to ease the passage of a tight-fitting ball down a rifle barrel. Patching also reduced powder fouling, thus somewhat protecting the bore and enhancing accuracy. European riflemen were soon killing deer and chamois at ranges considered impossible by smoothbore shooters. Some of the evidence concerning early target matches is dubious or contradictory, but a 1498 match at

Leipzig may possibly have included a special event for riflemen. During the next few centuries, European rulers financed shooting matches (and often provided fine prizes), partly in order to encourage shooting skill among citizens—potential soldiers in case of war—partly as a show of strength, and partly as a festive occasion for friendly competition and international neighborliness in the cause of peace. At first, the arms used were wheel locks with straight buttstocks—"cheek butts." By 1700 the new French-style flintlock had replaced the vastly inferior wheel lock, and the butts had become broader, smoother, and angled downward with enough drop for holding a rifle to the shoulder in pretty much the way a rifle is held and aimed today. Out of hunting and target competition had come the jaeger.

It was a short, .60- to .75-caliber rifle, usually with seven to nine deep, relatively slow-twisting grooves in a barrel from about 24 to 30 inches long. The stock, though it might be adorned with carving, was smooth where it touched the cheek, and on the right side, a rectangular box was carved into it and supplied with a sliding lid of wood, bone, ivory or horn, held closed by a spring catch. The bead front and open-notch rear sights were fairly crude by modern standards, but far better than anything previously devised. And most of these rifles had double-set triggers—the first trigger to set the mechanism, the second to produce let-off with a mere touch. The long, stiff trigger pull of an ordinary flintlock was not conducive to fine accuracy; the hair trigger of the jaeger was. European hunters carrying jaegers regularly brought home the wild bacon, and jaeger marksmen regularly took the coveted prizes at offhand matches where 3½-foot targets were set up at ranges of 800 feet or more.

These were the first rifles to have a significant impact on American shooting. They came chiefly to Pennsylvania, with

Jaeger rifle, direct forerunner of the Kentucky. It has a typically short—30-inch—octagonal barrel and sliding flint-and-patch-box cover. German colonists introduced it, and Pennsylvania gunsmiths soon devised modifications leading to the first truly American-designed rifle.

Fine Kentucky rifle signed and dated—"N. Kile–1817." It has a set trigger, handsomely-figured wood and elaborate patch-box cover.

the German immigrants of the early 18th century. Among those settlers were gunsmiths who began to modify their wares to fit local needs and conditions. Powder and lead, mostly imported from Europe, were scarce, expensive, and cumbersome to carry in quantity for days at a time in the forests of the frontier. In order to consume less ammunition, the gunsmiths gradually reduced bore sizes, and to make the powder charges burn more efficiently, they lengthened the barrels—a change that also improved accuracy by lengthening the sighting radius. But a longer rifle meant considerably more weight, so the stock was thinned down until it assumed a light, graceful form as handsome as it was functional. American woods were used, of course, and maple—particularly curly maple—became popular for its beautiful grain as well as its toughness. The sliding cover of the flint-and-patch box (which later became a cap-and-patch box) was replaced by a hinged brass or iron cover that could not be dropped and lost. It was carefully inletted into the stock so that its surface was smoothly level with the wood. Each little change brought the rifle closer to perfection for its time, place, and purposes. With improvement came increased pride of manufacture and ownership, and with pride came added refinements—improved cheekpieces, carving, and silver or brass inlays. What emerged was at first differentiated from the European rifle, or jaeger, by the simple name long rifle, or American rifle.

The barrel continued to grow—sometimes reaching a length of 46 inches in post-Revolutionary specimens—while the caliber was reduced to .60, then to about .50, and eventually to .40 or occasionally even less. The .50-caliber type was found to be powerful enough for deer and black bear, the largest game commonly found in the part of the continent that had so far been settled. It was powerful enough for use against Indians and Redcoats, as well, and accurate enough for shooting at targets or small game.

Informal shooting matches, which quickly gained popular-

Target shooting was widespread in early America, where a family's subsistence often depended upon marksmanship, as exemplified by George Caleb Bingham's "Shooting for the Beef."

ity in frontier America, have been celebrated in early literature and in such famous paintings as George Caleb Bingham's "Shooting for the Beef," Tompkins H. Matteson's "Turkey Shoot" (based on characters and an incident in James Fenimore Cooper's *The Pioneers*) and John W. Ehninger's "The Turkey Shoot" (a later work depicting shooters in 1879, some of whom are portrayed with weapons still resembling the old long rifles).

As for hunting, there are innumerable tales of impressive big-game shots with the long rifle, and almost as many concerning accuracy on small game. The great naturalist-artist John James Audubon once wrote about a Kentucky squirrel hunt on which he accompanied Daniel Boone. Audubon, who was a good shot, was impressed by Boone's skill at "barking" squirrels—aiming not at the animals but at the limbs on which they perched, killing them by concussion without spoiling an ounce of meat. The importance of food bestowed a proportionate importance on marksmanship. James Fenimore Cooper observed that "the ancient amusement of shooting the Christmas turkey is one of the few sports that the settlers of a new country seldom . . . neglect to observe." And a modern historian, Thomas

Fleming, has noted that frontier families counted on a holiday fare of freshly killed venison, bear steak, or turkey, because the unlucky or unskillful "might have to dig into the pork barrel, where they kept the salted meat on which they largely depended throughout the winter." In frontier America, a man who shot poorly was likely to be a poor man.

In warfare, too, American marksmen displayed a startling prowess with their long rifles. Britain had used jaeger riflemen as snipers in some of the continental wars of the 18th century, and a few troops were equipped with them again in America during the French and Indian War of 1755-1763. But during that war, the American long-riflemen so impressed the British that they began training special units to emulate the Colonials. When the Revolution erupted, Great Britain again employed jaegers, in the hands of Hessian mercenaries who sometimes proved deadly with them even at dusk—as they did in 1781 during the siege of Yorktown, for example. But again the Americans with their long rifles were, in general, even deadlier. Both sides relied chiefly on muskets, since rifles were still slow to load, and as

Tompkins H. Matteson's "Turkey Shoot," painted to illustrate an incident described by James Fenimore Cooper in his novel of American frontier life, The Pioneers.

Jacklighting deer from a boat—a deadly (and legal) hunting method in the 19th century, when riflemen paid less attention to new notions of sportsmanship than to the need for food. Yet even then, hunters with foresight were beginning to press for conservation.

a rule were not equipped with bayonets, the most important weapons in the mass close-quarters attacks of 18th century warfare. But some Americans could not obtain muskets, and a few preferred the accuracy of the rifle to the speed and the bayonet of the musket.

As the newly organized Continental Army marched to Cambridge in 1775, some of the soldiers enjoyed showing the town dwellers along the way how woodsmen could shoot. One Virginian was said to have capped the astonishment by putting eight consecutive shots into a five-by-seven-inch mark at a range of 60 yards.

Major George Hanger, a British officer captured by American riflemen at the battle of Saratoga, in 1777, afterward reported: "I am certain that provided an American rifleman was to get a perfect aim at 300 yards at me standing still, he most undoubtedly would hit me, unless it was a very windy day."

Also at the Battle of Saratoga, an American marksman named Tim Murphy was supposed to have used a double-barreled long rifle made by John Golcher of Easton, Pennsylvania, to shoot down British General Simon Fraser at a range of at least 200 yards. The story of General Frazer's death is extremely dubious at best—it was perpetuated on the basis of hearsay by a 19th-century amateur historian named Benson J. Lossing—yet it is significant if only because experienced marksmen of the time had no reason to disbelieve it. British muskets were expected to hit a man-sized target consistently at no more than 80 yards, while American riflemen were enjoying shooting matches in which they had to hit the heads of turkeys—offhand at 250 feet, with rests at 350 feet.

In October 1780, at the Battle of Kings Mountain in the Carolinas, more than 1100 American Tories under Major Patrick Ferguson, an able Scots soldier, were surprised by a force of 900 backwoods Patriots. The Rebels crept up through the rocky woods surrounding the plateau, fighting in Indian style, picking off individual targets. When Ferguson ordered a bayonet charge, the American riflemen melted back into the forest fringes and continued sniping from long range. Ferguson was killed, and within an hour the Tories surrendered; 250 of them had been killed, 163 wounded, 715 taken prisoner. Of the American riflemen, only 28 were killed and 63 wounded.

The last great fight in which the long rifle figured significantly was the Battle of New Orleans at the close of the War

Maynard tape primer on rifled musket built shortly before the Civil War.

HARPER'S WEEKLY.

A JOURNAL OF CIVILIZATION.

VOL. V.—No. 249.]   NEW YORK, SATURDAY, OCTOBER 5, 1861.   [SINGLE COPIES SIX CENTS.
$2.50 PER YEAR IN ADVANCE.

Entered according to Act of Congress, in the Year 1861, by Harper & Brothers, in the Clerk's Office of the District Court for the Southern District of New York.

THE NEW HAMPSHIRE SHARP-SHOOTERS.—[See Page 636.]

of 1812. Like so many battles, it was a useless carnage, fought only because neither side had received word that the war had ended. Artillery and smoothbores were important in the engagement, but so were the rifles carried by General Andrew Jackson's force of Tennessee and Kentucky woodsmen. The British suffered 2600 casualties, the Americans just 13.

A ballad celebrating the needless and bloody victory quickly became popular. Its lyrics praised the "hunters of Kentucky and their Kentucky rifles." Most such rifles had at first come from Pennsylvania's Lancaster County. By the time of the Revolution, they were being made in York, Reading, Philadelphia, Pittsburgh, and various parts of Maryland, Virginia, New York and New England. By the time of the War of 1812, they were also coming from Ohio, Tennessee and the Carolinas, as well as Kentucky. But the name Kentucky rifle was permanently impressed on the public consciousness, and that has always remained the most common name for the American long rifle.

For generations it was the nation's outstanding meat-harvesting tool, and an important implement of entertainment. It was rivaled only by the shotgun—or perhaps only by the relatively short, handy, double-barreled class of shotguns that became practical in the early 19th century as a result of design improvements contributed by the English gunsmiths Henry Nock and Joseph Manton. Even today, a writer must be cautious about using the past tense in describing the illustrious life of the Kentucky rifle, for a number of master gunsmiths still build arms of the same type, and a number of hunters—black-powder aficionados—still use these and other muzzleloaders to take game.

The Kentucky rifle bridged the transition from flintlock to percussion ignition—the great scent-bottle percussion lock and subsequent caplock firing system originated by the Reverend Alexander John Forsyth, an estimable clergyman and duck hunter of Aberdeenshire, Scotland. The percussion system gained ascendancy quickly in the United States, and was just as quickly eclipsed by a breechloading design that employed self-primed ammunition and facilitated the perfection of repeaters—

Page from October 5, 1861 issue of Harper's Weekly *depicting Union sharpshooters using heavy-barreled rifles with telescopic sights. Some features of these rifles were soon used in* Schuetzen *rifles for offhand matches, and in very heavy slug-shooting bench-rest rifles.*

the rifles described by awe-stricken Civil War soldiers as guns that could be "loaded on Sunday and fired all week."

In 1848 an inventive genius named Walter Hunt (who had already perfected a safety pin and a sewing machine) developed a hollow-based, powder-containing bullet, and the following year he patented a rifle for it, the Volitional Repeater. It had a trigger-guard operating lever and a tubular magazine with a follower spring to chamber successive loads. He sold the rights to a machinist named George Arrowsmith, who employed a fine designer, Lewis Jennings, to improve the mechanism. Then the rights were re-sold, and the Vermont firm of Robbins & Lawrence began production. At this stage, the rifle was examined by Horace Smith and Daniel Wesson, the famous gun-making partners, each of whom further refined it. In 1854 they began producing rifles at a Connecticut plant, after founding the Vol-

Mid-19th century painting—one of a series entitled American Frontier Life—*by Arthur F. Tait. The horseman's rifle looks like a transitional piece, with features of both the Kentucky and the plains rifle.*

Frederic Remington drawing of a 19th-century Texan. His firearm looks like a typical Hawken—the classic plains rifle.

canic Repeating Arms Company. One of the 40 investors was a New Haven shirt manufacturer, Oliver Fisher Winchester.

Gradually, Winchester—a skillful financier, administrator and promotor of new products—acquired controlling interest. In 1858 he assigned a mechanic and designer named Benjamin Tyler Henry to devise a safe, powerful, self-contained cartridge. The result was the metal-cased .44 rimfire, which has been characterized by the arms historian Harold L. Peterson as "a fantastic advance in ammunition design." Its 216-grain bullet was lighter than most bullets of that era, and its 26-grain charge of black powder was relatively small, yet it had a muzzle velocity of 1200 feet per second.

Henry revamped the Volcanic rifle to handle his cartridge, simultaneously improving the locking bolt and remodeling the firing pin to reduce the chance of misfires. In government tests, the 16-shot Henry repeater proved to be a marvel: It could fire 120 shots in five minutes and forty seconds, including loading and reloading time—an average of one shot every 2.9 seconds. Patented in 1860, it was ready to be marketed in 1862. Ironically, the Federal Government bought fewer than 1800 of the new rifles, and not many were used during the Civil War, while the

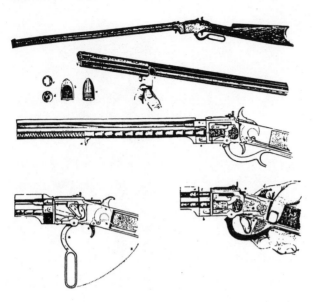

Diagrams from Frank Leslie's Illustrated Newspaper *showing the then-new Volcanic Repeating Rifle.*

Union purchased far greater numbers of Spencer repeaters—lever-actions patented just before the Henry. Cheaper and somewhat sturdier than the original Henry, they had the disadvantage of requiring manual cocking for every shot, but they could be loaded very quickly, and they handled larger bullets, which were then thought to be more deadly than the .44. After the war, however, a trend toward smaller, higher-velocity calibers favored the Henry, as did its 16 shots. The Spencer held only seven. A new, sturdier version, the Winchester Model 1866—also called the Yellow Boy in reference to the bright brass frame of the first rifles produced—won the favor of the public.

Three years later the Spencer Repeating Rifle Company was out of business, while Winchester continued to undergo improvements and soaring popularity. There is some question as to whether it, or any other single model, accurately could be designated "The Gun That Won the West" (a slogan composed many years later), but comparable tributes were paid it by Indians who called it the "heap-firing gun," "many-shots" and—greatest praise of all—the "spirit-gun."

It was prized by lawmen, soldiers, hunters and everyone else who had need of a rifle, particularly after it was chambered for a succession of new cartridges. Soon the West was supplied

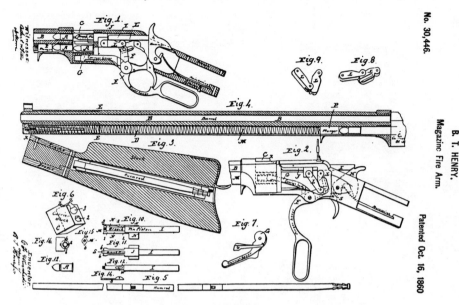

One of the patent drawings for the Henry rifle.

with a great many Winchesters, as well as more or less similar lever actions of other makes, although it is probably safe to say that such quick-handling, fast-firing, open-sighted rifles and carbines enjoyed their greatest and most practical use in Eastern timber hunting for deer and black bear. Even today, the descendants of those Winchesters are among the most popular arms for such hunting.

But the highly accurate, powerful, long-range, single-shot rifle was not sacrificed on the altar of repeat fire. The demise of the Kentucky rifle was roughly concurrent with the rise of the full-stocked and half-stocked plains rifles, or Hawkens. In heavier, shorter form, they combined the basic lines of the Kentucky rifle with the economy and simplicity of the trade gun. Early barrel lengths ran up to about 42 inches, later ones averaged between 28 and 38 inches, and calibers ranged from about .42 to .60, but with a .50 and .53 gaining the greatest popularity, particularly among buffalo hunters. They were made by Henry Deringer (of pocket-pistol fame) and many other gunsmiths from Philadelphia to St. Louis, and later in such widely distant regions as Illinois and Colorado. Foremost among the plains-rifle makers were the brothers Jacob and Samuel Hawken, heirs of a gun-making family from Pennsylvania and Maryland who

Man in the foreground of John Clymer's painting Gold
Train *is carrying a Henry rifle, forerunner of the first
Winchester lever-action, the Model 1866.*

established a shop in the frontier town of St. Louis. Their guns
and others of the same type were used by all the famous mountain men, including Jim Bridger, Kit Carson and Joe Meek.

In the 1890's, the noted marksman Horace Kephart bought
one from a St. Louis dealer, and he commented on it in a *Saturday Evening Post* article in 1920. Firing half-ounce lead balls,
Kephart found that he could keep all of his shots inside 12 inches
at 200 yards. And that was with the rifle's original open sights—
a silver-bead front and a buckhorn rear.

Back East, shooting matches continued to be popular, and
they included the German and Swiss-style festivals—*Schuetzenfests*. Gallons of beer, great mounds of sauerbraten, and many
pounds of lead and powder were consumed at those contests.
Social clubs called *Bunds* or *Vereins* were organized by the German communities in New York and as far west as Chicago and
Milwaukee. The first national *Schuetzenfest* was held in New
York the year after the Civil War ended. A festival's major
event was usually an offhand contest at long range—200 yards
as a rule. And for this specialized kind of shooting, a heavy,

octagonal-barreled single-shot rifle—the *Schuetzen* rifle—was developed.

The most popular bore sizes ranged from .32 to .45. Weight generally ranged from 12 to 16 pounds. Detachable false muzzles were used on some to protect the rifling when a ball was started down the bore (though late-vintage *Schuetzens* were often breechloaders). The front sight was usually a bead, sometimes protectively hooded, and the rear was an aperture, often minutely adjustable. (Telescopic sights had been used by Berdan's Sharpshooters during the Civil War, and they continued in use, particularly in Germany, but their real popularity began with the rise of chuck-shooting as an American sport during the early 20th century.) An optional but common *Schuetzen* feature was a hinged, adjustable palm rest, attached to the forestock or barrel as a support for the forward hand. The buttstock was broad, with a deeply curved metal buttplate that had long "horns" at the heel and toe, designed to pass over the rifleman's shoulder and under his arm for extra steadiness. Most *Schuetzens,* especially the early ones, were custom-built, but before the century ended, companies like Winchester, Marlin, Sharps and Remington were supplying these arms for the popular competitions. And at last, shortly after 1900, scopes were permitted for specified events. The accuracy of these rifles was comparable to that of the Creedmoor and other such long-range match rifles of the period. If the first World War had not aroused a strong bias against all things German, *Schuetzenfests* undoubtedly would have remained popular for another generation or even more.

Meanwhile, back in 1873, an Irish rifle team had won the great English Wimbledon match, a celebrated ultra-long-range competition. And then they had sent a challenge overseas to the "Riflemen of America," a challenge printed in the newspapers. In response, a group called the Amateur Rifle Club was formed to hold competitions and select an American team. Two American gun companies, Remington and Sharps, contributed prize funds and designed rifles for the purpose. One model was based on the standard Sharps falling-block action; the other was designed by Lewis Hepburn on the Remington rolling-block action. Both were slender, graceful single-shot rifles with hooded front sights and adjustable vernier and wind-gauge rear aperture sights. On September 26, 1874, at the new Creedmoor Range on Long Island, the eight American shooters vied with the eight Irish marksmen, each firing 15 shots at 800 yards, 15 at 900, and

15 at 1000. The targets were standard Wimbledon rectangles, 12 feet wide, 6 feet high, with a three-foot-square bull's-eye inside a six-by-six-foot center area. The final score was 934 to 931. The Americans won.

For years after that, Creedmoor and Creedmoor-style rifles were prized possessions among marksmen, and shooting matches ranging from the *Schuetzenfest* to the Creedmoor-Wimbledon type were extremely popular. But the World War curtailed civilian shooting. Even contests that had no trace of German influence waned, despite private and governmental campaigns to encourage civilian marksmanship. And years passed before long-range shooting contests again became popular at such meccas as Camp Perry, under the aegis of the National Rifle Association, the various military teams, the Olympic committees, the Pan American organizations and similar groups. Fortunately, today's array of rifle-shooting events is larger than ever, encompassing both rim-fire and center-fire competitions, events fired at many distances, events using metal game silhouettes and running-boar as well as stationary targets, and matches involving many kinds of arms, from single-shot free rifles to bolt actions and semiautomatic military rifles.

One other kind of rifle competition—bench-rest shooting—also received great impetus in 19th-century America. Many authorities date the rise of modern bench-rest shooting from the early 1930's, but it really began in the mid-1800's, at first as a method of testing rifle barrels, rather than as a competition. Soon it became a noncompetitive diversion for gun enthusiasts who were interested in ballistics and mechanics, and then quickly developed into a form of competitive shooting. In the 1850's Sir Joseph Whitworth introduced a new metal for gun barrels, called fluid compressed steel, and many of the best English and American barrelmakers adopted this steel. American makers such as Morgan James, H.V. Perry, Horace

One of Buffalo Bill Cody's "show guns"—an elegant 1873 Winchester rifle with an engraved receiver and fancy wood.

A contemporary drawing for a news account of the great 1874 Irish-American rifle match at Creedmoor, Long Island. It was America's answer to Wimbledon; the American team won.

Warner, and N.S. Brockway built "bench rifles" with heavy barrels of the improved steel. A somewhat lighter scoped version built by Edwin Wesson was used by some Union sharpshooters during the Civil War.

The early bench-rest rifles were generally heavy-barreled percussion pieces employing false muzzles, a cross paper patch, a bullet starter, set triggers, a hooded pin-head from sight and a finely adjustable vernier aperture rear sight. They fired big cylindro-conoidal slugs with heavy charges of black powder. For a while, matches with these fine target arms were established in parts of the Northeast, but their popularity did not spread, and the sport waned until the 1930's.

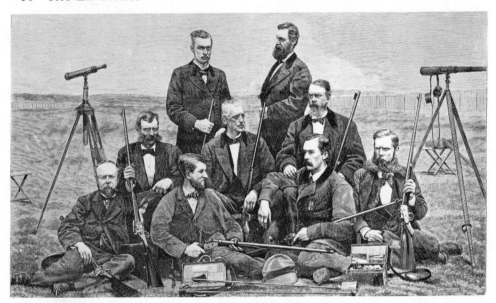

Harper's Weekly *portrait of the riflemen who captured the world's long-range championship for the United States in 1874.*

An Americanized Schuetzenfest, *fired with standard rifles rather than match-quality* Schuetzens, *at a public shooting range in the late 1860's.*

In the intervening years, however, advances were made in the rifles and their ammunition. By the turn of the century, Dr. Franklin W. Mann was experimenting with barrels provided by Harry Pope and other famous makers, and in 1909 he published a book entitled *The Bullet's Flight from Powder to Target*. It was subtitled *The Internal and External Ballistics of Small Arms* and was described on the title page as "a study of rifle shooting with the personal element excluded, disclosing the cause of the error at target." Some of Dr. Mann's shooting was done from supports, rather like modern machine rests, to reduce the "human element" almost totally. During the same period, of course, arms manufacturers were developing sophisticated apparatus and techniques for comparable purposes. Such experiments, as well as more conventional bench-rest shooting, provided an excellent test of barrels, actions, and new types of ammunition; these trials—of the equipment rather than the shooter —were invaluable to the improvement of rifles, cartridges, powder, and bullets.

Even before the turn of the century, smokeless-powder experiments were being conducted in England and France, and in this country by such firms as Winchester, Remington, Savage, Union Metallic Cartridge Company and others. Improvements in ammunition—hence, in accuracy, safety, power and controlled effects at the target or during penetration of game— have appeared steadily ever since.

So have innovations in rifle actions. It can be claimed that the modern bolt-action originated in France in 1829, with the patent of the needle-fire mechanism by the Prussian, Jean Nicholas Von Dreyse; or in more modern form, it can be dated from the 1860 rifle of Peter Paul Mauser or the still later, improved versions introduced by the United States during the Spanish American War. Perhaps no mechanism has ever equalled the bolt action for combining hunting accuracy with ease, speed, and reliability of operation. For that matter, the bolt action has achieved success even in the most demanding target versions. As for the various semiautomatic designs, they can all be traced to American inventiveness, specifically to the inventive efforts begun in the 1880's by the arms-making genius John Moses Browning. The pump, or slide action, too, originated with Browning. His design, which first enjoyed commercial success in the Model 1897 Winchester exposed-hammer shotgun, has since been modified for use in many rifles and smoothbores. Like so many other advances in arms design, both the semiauto-

*Author sighting in modern, scoped bolt-action rifle with .264
Winchester Magnum hand loads prior to mule-deer hunt. Rifle
delivered clean, one-shot kill.*

Opposite, above
*Modern bench-rest champion, Mrs. Mary Louise DeVito,
smiling happily after scoring the world record for 1000 yards—
a group measuring 7^{11}/$_{16}$ inches—at the Original
Pennsylvania 1000-Yard Bench Rest Club. Custom-built rifle
had a 30-inch Hart barrel; cartridge was a 7mm/300 Weatherby
wildcat. Such competitions have been soaring in popularity
since the 1930's.*

Opposite, below
*Martin J. Hull, ballistics engineer for Sierra bullets, firing
custom-built 7.62 NATO (.308 Winchester) target rifle at 1970
Palma Trophy Match in England. Top American competitor,
Hull fired high score of match—219X225—at 800, 900 and
1000 yards.*

matic and the slide action were developed not to vanquish nations on the battlefields but to meet the needs of American
sportsmen.

Without any fear of accusations about nationalistic bias, it
can be asserted that modern rifles and rifle marksmanship have
had their greatest impetus, made their most impressive advances, and reached their highest levels in America. It has always been a nation of marksmen.

Calibers and Ammunition for Big Game

Bob Hagel

In discussing big game cartridges and loads for shooting American game, it is probably best to consider the various classes of game, and the conditions under which they will be hunted. To do this, generalizing some on the different species and hunting conditions, we can form two classes of game by animal size, and two types of hunting conditions. As for size or weight class, the smallest would be deer-size game, which can logically include everything from antelope to mule deer of the ungulates, as well as black bears that usually fall into the same weight class, and are normally killed by deer hunters. The second class would include all of the other species from caribou to moose and Alaskan brown bears. There will be some hunters who will not agree with including caribou in the heavy class of game, and they may have a point for a couple of reasons; some sub-species of caribou are not too much larger than a big buck muley, and they are not generally considered to be especially hard to kill. The reason for including them in the heavy game bracket here is that in many areas in both Alaska and Canada, big bulls will run nearly as heavy as cow elk. And even though they are not especially hard to kill, as compared to some other game, they are often hunted in the same places (the Alaska Peninsula being an example) and shot on the same day as moose and grizzly, or the larger Alaskan brown bears. It follows that the rifle used on a general-bag Alaskan or Canadian hunt should be chambered for a cartridge suited to moose and big bear hunting, but will also be used for caribou.

Even though antelope are included in the deer-size weight class, there is a difference in the hunting which, while it does not make many good deer cartridges unsuitable, it does make certain cartridges much more desirable for antelope shooting. The rea-

34

son for this being that more pronghorn are shot at longer range than any other American game animal. It is often possible to stalk nearer to antelope than most hunters do, but there are many times when the shot *must* be fired at long range or not at all. And if that shot is at a record-book buck, most hunters will try it.

An antelope buck is not as large as most deer, a big buck weighing about 100 pounds, but is still as large as some whitetail sub-species found in the Southwest, and not a great deal smaller than the Sitka blacktail of coastal Alaska. Certainly any cartridge that is potent enough to kill deer will have plenty of punch for antelope, but that doesn't make it a good antelope cartridge. On the other hand, good antelope cartridges are also good deer cartridges, and, if the right bullet design and weight are used for the kind of game hunted, some are also good for elk, moose and big bears.

As they are small, it doesn't take much penetration to reach the vital organs of an antelope from any angle. For broadside lung shots, any of the high velocity .22 cartridges with the heavier bullet weights from 55-70 grains will make quick kills in most instances. But anyone who has hunted and shot many antelope knows that for every perfect broadside shot at a standing antelope, several more are taken, with a hit *anywhere* resulting more from luck than good shooting. For that reason (and the fact that .22 caliber bullets, even though they start at very high velocity, soon lose much of the velocity), larger caliber bullets of heavier weight from .243 up, and started at nearly equal velocities, are reliable under *all* antelope hunting conditions. Consequently, we won't even consider the .22 cartridges as being adequate in the hands of the average hunter even for pronghorn hunting.

What is needed for antelope hunting is high velocity with a bullet of high ballistic coefficient to give the flattest possible trajectory over all reasonable ranges, which for the average hunter is no more than 400 yards. I know a lot of stories are told around the fire about 600 to 1000 yard antelope kills, but when it does happen even at the nearer range, it is mostly accidental. And if you don't believe that, put up a silhouette target of an antelope at 600 yards or farther, and see how often you can put a hole in the vital lung/shoulder area from hunting positions—especially with the first shot! The fact is, not every sporter is capable of the accuracy it takes to lay all of its bullets in the 10- to 11-inch vital area, even if the hunter is, which is also doubtful.

Anyway, a good antelope cartridge should get its bullets out to 400 yards with the least possible drop, and from a rifle that has the kind of accuracy it takes to keep them all in a 10-inch circle. Those bullets must also be structured so that they will expand every time, whether they hit the pronghorn in the lungs, shoulder, paunch or ham. For this reason, the jacket must be thin at the point, but should be heavy enough farther back so that it does not explode to the degree where it fails to give sufficient penetration. This rules out the bullets made with varmint shooting as the criterion—those bullets are made to explode on very small targets with little resistance.

Except for the fact that bullets used especially for antelope hunting can be a bit lighter in weight and expand a bit faster and to a greater degree, the same cartridges that prove ideal for antelope are also excellent for any deer-size game at long range. Remember that a big buck mule deer, and some whitetails, or a trophy ram or billy goat, will outweigh a big antelope buck by as much as three to one. For that reason, when using any of the .243 caliber cartridges as an example, most bullets of from 85–105 grains will do very well for pronghorn, but in using the same caliber cartridges for deer, sheep or goat, the 100-grain factory load and hand load with the various 100-grain spitzer bullets, the 105-grain Speer or the 95-grain Nosler Partition are preferred. The 85-grain Nosler Partition will also give sufficient penetration on the larger animals from most any angle, but has poor long-range form.

The same thing can be said for the .25 and 6.5mm cartridges. The lighter bullets in the .25 cartridges that are designed with big game in mind, from 87-100 grain, are fine for pronghorn, but the 100-120 grain bullets will perform better on game like mule deer in all hunting situations. In 6.5mm cartridges, the 100-grain bullet will do quite well on antelope, even though it is overly explosive in most brands, and the 120- to 125-grain bullets are ideal. But for the larger deer-size game, the 120 to 140-grain bullets are preferred for long-range work.

Moving up to the .270, either Winchester or the more potent Weatherby, the light bullets of 90-100 grains are made for varmint shooting, and while they will kill antelope well with broadside hits, they are overly destructive. In fact, for antelope and all other deer-size game, the 130 grain is ideal. It shoots flat, is usually very accurate, and has plenty of velocity even in the .270 Winchester to expand well at long range on antelope, yet give plenty of penetration on the largest deer from any angle. The .270 Winchester is perhaps one of the most popular cartridges

These cartridges will take care of most hunting situations for the majority of American game, if used within their effective range, and if the bullet used is designed for the game being shot. From left: .308 Winchester, 7×57 Mauser, .270 Winchester, .280 Remington, 30-06, 7mm Remington Magnum, .300 Winchester Magnum and .338 Winchester Magnum.

for long-range hunting of deer-size game, and with good reason; it has proven itself over a long period of hunting time.

Most gun-buffs are probably aware that I have killed a great deal of varied game with 7mm caliber cartridges, from the 7×57 Mauser to the ultra-velocity wildcat magnums, and all of these make top-rate long-range cartridges for shooting any class of American hoofed game. I've killed a number of antelope with a 7×57 loaded up to where it belongs in a good bolt action, as well as some with the larger capacity 7mm cartridges like the 7mm Mashburn Super Magnum, and performance is superb. The lighter bullets of 139-150 grains are best for antelope, and work equally well on the larger deer-size game. My personal preference for bullets in the magnum cases is something like the Nosler that stays in one piece at all hunting ranges. Light thin-skinned bullets started at 7mm magnum velocities are pretty hard on eating-meat. The fact is, the heavier 160-grain spitzer bullets are as good or better in the magnum cases as lighter bullets. When started at plus 3100 fps, they have few peers for long-range shooting of everything from pronghorn to elk.

Most mountain grizzlies are shot in Alaska and Western Canada in open country like this timberline. For this kind of shooting, where game isn't likely to get out of sight or to get to the hunter before other shots can be fired, anything from the .270 Winchester up with the right bullet will give good results. This one was killed by the writer in the Alaska Range with a 300 Winchester Model 70 and 200-grain Nosler, an ideal big-bear load.

There have probably been more deer killed with .30 caliber bullets than any other, but that doesn't make most .30 caliber cartridges the best choice for long-range shooting on deer-class game. Certainly no .30 caliber cartridge that churns up less velocity than the .308 Winchester can be considered as a good bet for long-range shooting of any kind. With factory ammunition, it is not ideal even with the lighter bullet weights, but with hand loads in a strong bolt action, the 150-grain bullet can be started at about 2900 fps, and the 125-130 grain at 3100 fps with the right powders. With that velocity, the .308 will do quite well at ranges to 350 yards without doing too much guessing where the bullet will land. The venerable old .30-06 will add near 200 fps to those velocity figures, if loaded to its full potential in modern bolt actions, but again, factory ammunition is badly underloaded because of the many different types of actions of questionable strength for which it is chambered. As a sidelight, I have never chronographed any factory 180-grain .30-06 load that gave the 2700 fps in a hunting rifle the ballistic data sheets show. Some brands show less than 2600 fps! However, with full-throttle loads and the lighter bullets up to 180 grains, the old cartridge delivers good long-range results on all deer-size game, and you don't have to feel embarrassed in any company on the antelope flats.

While the .30 magnums are considered to be needlessly powerful for antelope and deer at any range, they are superb cartridges for any long-range shooting on all hoofed game. The problem here is that not everyone can handle the recoil of a big .30 well enough to shoot it accurately at long range from hunting positions. If you can handle it, the fact that cartridges like the .308 Norma, the .300 Winchester and the .300 Weatherby will

Mature bull elk are big animals and require bullets that give deep penetration when they are shot in timber in all positions and at various angles. This one was killed with a .300 Winchester Model 70 and 180-grain Nosler that shattered shoulder and spine, then made exit.

kick a 180-grain bullet along at well over 3100 fps, the 165-grain at 3300 fps and the 150-grain at plus 3400 fps will eliminate much of the guesswork of where to hold at long range.

In summing up the various cartridges mentioned for long-range shooting of game from antelope to mule deer, it is obvious that the potential of the cartridge hinges on velocity. Surely accuracy is as important as velocity, but any cartridge has plenty of accuracy if you use the right load in it, so the main factor becomes the rifle. This being true, the higher velocity the cartridge develops in any given caliber with the same bullet weight, the more desirable it is as a long-range cartridge. The less drop the bullet has, the more chance you have of putting it in the right spot at unknown ranges. Also, the more velocity the bullet retains out where the game is, the more reliable expansion will be, and if a bullet fails to expand, killing effect will be very low. Considering all of this, and even though you may be biased toward a "pet" cartridge, there is little doubt that the magnum

Muley buck, shot with 6mm Remington and 95-grain Nosler bullet. This is an ideal cartridge/bullet combination for all deer-size game at all reasonable hunting ranges. This one was shot as he lay in his bed on far side of canyon at 350 yards.

Even a mature buck antelope is a small animal weighing only about 100 pounds, and the vital heart/lung area is only about 11" in diameter. Being shot at longer ranges than any other American big game on an average, high accuracy and flat trajectory, coupled with a bullet that expands well at the longest game ranges, are extremely important to successful pronghorn hunting.

cases in all calibers will give better long-range performance than the smaller cases.

In .243 caliber cartridges, the .240 Weatherby holds the edge over the .243 Winchester and the 6mm Remington. By the same token, the .264 Winchester Magnum shoots flatter than the various 6.5mm cartridges of foreign origin, or the 6.5mm Remington Magnum, which really isn't a magnum capacity case. The .270 Weatherby steps along much faster than the .270 Winchester, and the various 7mm magnums outclass the 7×57 Mauser, .280 Remington and .284 Winchester for speed and less bullet drop. The big .30's also get their bullets to the far side of a sheep basin or across a sage-flat with less drop than the smaller cartridges. It is as simple as that.

When we think of hunting deer-size game in thick cover, game like sheep, goats and antelope are automatically elimi-

While caribou are not especially hard to kill, they are usually shot with powerful cartridges because they are normally hunted in connection with larger game like moose, mountain grizzly and Alaskan brown bear. This bull killed on an Alaskan Peninsula hunt by writer's hunting partner, Jake Jacobson, was upset with 7mm Remington Magnum and 175-grain Nosler. Jake weighs 250 pounds, so it is obvious that the bull is a big animal.

nated, so this leaves the various kinds of deer (whitetail, black-tail and mule deer) and black bears, more of which are killed by deer hunters while hunting deer than while looking for bears. Mule deer are often hunted in cover so thick that any whitetail would be right at home. And with hunting pressure increasing every year on most mountain mule deer ranges, they are acting more like whitetails—shunning the open hillsides in favor of the heavily timbered slopes.

It hasn't been so long since any deer hunter who didn't pack a .30-30, .32 Special or .35 Remington into the deer woods was considered strange. I can remember when there were many .25-

35's, .30-30's and .32 Specials used in hunting mule deer in the West. But in those days, there were a lot of deer to choose from, and a lot fewer hunters looking for them. Not so today. You'll find a lot more .243's, .308's, .270's and aught-sixes used in deer hunting in most places than .30-30's. There isn't anything wrong with the .30-30 class cartridge for shooting deer-size game in heavy cover, but there are many other cartridges that will work just as well. If you use a .243 or .25-06 for shooting deer in open country, there is no reason you shouldn't take it into the brush. Don't be mislead by the old tale that it takes a slow-moving, round-nose bullet to make a good cartridge for shooting deer in the brush because a pointed bullet at high velocity can't get through—neither can the slow round-nose if it hits anything larger than a leaf or small twig that is more than a dozen feet from the deer. There just isn't any such thing as a good "brush bucking" bullet. If you don't want to wound or miss a deer, or any other animal, make sure you pick an open spot to put the bullet through.

Another way of looking at it is that the high velocity cartridge is just as effective at close range in the brush as the .30-30,

Mountain goats are often shot at long range, so the ideal cartridge should have flat trajectory. The same cartridges would be ideal for all long-range shooting at deer-size game, including antelope, all deer, sheep and black bear.

but the .30-30 lacks what it takes to reliably hit and kill a buck on the other side of a canyon or meadow at 300 yards. The .30–30 class cartridge is very effective on deer if you know its range limitations and shoot accordingly—out to not over 200 yards. These cartridges do not ruin as much meat as the high velocity numbers at close range, which is something to consider. But if you use the heavier weight bullets, and especially those that have jackets designed to control expansion, a lot of the meat-spoilage problem will be solved. There is also another reason for using the heavier-weight bullets in the high-velocity cartridges for hunting in heavy cover, and that is that you seldom find the animal in an ideal position. It is more likely to be quartering to or from the gun from broadside, and in many cases, all you'll see is its rump rapidly disappearing among the trees. You'll need the extra penetration the heavier bullets afford to make certain they reach the vital organs from any direction.

As far as the hunting conditions are concerned, there is no difference in hunting elk and moose in thick cover than deer. The same adverse shooting conditions are there, the long angles and difficulty in being certain of what part of the animal you are looking at, and the problem of finding a clear hole to send the bullet through that is in line with the right spot on the bull at the right time. But the hunter's problem in making a clean, quick kill is multiplied many times by the size of the animal and the great amount of penetration it takes to reach the vital organs from these same long angles. I am well aware that the calm, cool and prudent hunter does not shoot unless he is certain of the spot he is shooting at and *thinks* he knows how the animal is standing, which would automatically eliminate all running shots. I also know that few hunters are that calm, cool and collected, except when they tell the story. And even if they do hold their fire until the game appears to be in the right position, they often find that the supposed broadside shot was fired from an angle, or with the animal in a twist, requiring the bullet to penetrate part of the paunch or heavy shoulder to get inside the lung cavity.

For these reasons it is hard to justify using small-caliber light bullets for shooting heavy game in the brush. The very minimum in bullet diameter is the .270, and then only with the 150- or, better yet, the 160-grain Nosler Partition bullets. With these bullets, penetration will be sufficient in most cases, but the wound channel is not overly large, and they do not pack the shock effect of the larger calibers. Personally, I don't like to hunt heavy game in the bushes with anything less than a 7mm with 175-grain bullets, and these should also be Noslers, because I know of no other bullet that will deliver that kind of sure bone-shattering penetration. And I like to fire them in one of the 7mm magnum cases. I've killed a number of elk with 160-grain Noslers at close quarters, but they are not as reliable as the 175's. Actually, if I know the hunting is going to be in heavy timber and brush, I prefer even larger calibers.

The 200-grain Nosler or the 220-grain Remington Core-Lokt will do a good job in .30 caliber cartridges, with the former being the best when loaded in magnum cases. However, the .30–06 will do a creditable job with either of these bullets loaded as hot as the cartridge will handle it for trouble-free hunting use. It is not that you need the velocity because of flatter trajectory, or that it will necessarily give deeper penetration, but because it tears up more vital nerves and tissue and gives greater shock to help anchor the animal near where it is hit.

As far as reliability for hunting heavy game in heavy timber is concerned, it is doubtful that any caliber surpasses the .388 bore. The .388 Winchester, the .340 Weatherby or any of the various wildcats give excellent results if the right bullets are used. Most of the 250- to 300-grain bullets will do a good job, but the 250-grain Nosler and the Bitterroot Bonded Core of the same weight (not available at the time this is written) will give deeper penetration than any of the others, and the 210-grain Nosler will do nearly as well.

Currently there are no really good .35 caliber bullets being made, as far as deep penetration is concerned, so this caliber is not as successful for hunting heavy game in the brush as it could be. Little needs to be said about the .375 cartridges for hunting heavy game, but even those powerful cartridges fall short if the bullets break up and fail to penetrate. I have used 300-grain bullets in both .33 and .375 caliber cartridges that expanded too much and failed to penetrate through the rib cavity on bull elk and moose broadside. On these same shots, a 150-grain Nosler from a .270 would have left an exit hole. A large caliber doesn't necessarily make it ideal for large game in the timber, but it is ideal if the right bullet is available and you use it.

Where long shots at elk and moose are likely to be necessary, the .270 is still probably the smallest caliber that should be considered, although a good 140-grain pointed bullet in the .264 Winchester will do the job if you place your shot right. In the .270, the pointed 150 grain is the best choice, with pointed 160- and 175-grain bullets in the 7mm cartridges the best. Pointed bul-

A big bull moose, like this one on the Alaskan Peninsula, is by far the heaviest animal hunted in North America, and it may be better to have too much gun than too little; many will not be in the ideal broadside position this bull presents.

lets of no more than 200 grains are the answer in the .30 caliber cartridges, and the 210-grain Nosler, 225-grain Hornady and 250-grain Sierra BT are top choices for the .338 and .340. As elk and moose are both big and may not be broadside for the shot even though they are in the open and standing, a bullet of strong jacket construction is highly desirable, especially in the lighter weights mentioned.

For all-around hunting of heavier game where the shots may be taken in the timber at nose-rubbing distances, or in the open where they may be as far as you and your cartridge are capable of a clean kill, the cartridges mentioned for long-range shooting are the best choice, and with the bullets in pointed form with strong jacket structure. In fact, the same cartridges and bullets are the ideal compromise for mixed-bag hunting in areas where deer-size game and larger game will be hunted on the same trip and often killed on the same day. An example of this is in the Mountain States where mule deer and elk are very often found in the same area. A tough 180-grain spitzer bullet in a .30-06 or .300 magnum will give flat trajectory for the long shots at either animal, and will penetrate quite well on the elk even at close range in the brush. The same situation is the rule in western Canada and Alaska, with sheep, goat, black bear and caribou on the light-game side, and moose and grizzly on the heavy end. Here the same cartridge/bullet compromise will be effective. My own preference is even stronger toward the magnum cartridges for hunting in the North, where the moose are very large and grizzly and brown bears have been known to get nasty if the first shot didn't put them out of commission. If you don't need the extra range and punch the big cartridges give, you haven't lost anything; if you do need it, you have it. If there is such a thing as "overkill," it doesn't hurt anything.

A chapter on cartridges and loads for hunting American game wouldn't be complete without a short look at shooting the big bears. Probably the majority of mountain grizzlies are shot in open country above timberline in the North. For this kind of shooting, where the hunter usually stalks the bear and has plenty

This Dall ram was killed at 400 yards with .300 Winchester Model 70 and 180-grain Nosler backed by 79-grain H4831 at 3150 fps. That same load stopped a charging grizzly at five feet. The bullet expanded well on the ram at 400 yards, yet smashed the shoulder of the grizzly, and made exit near the flank at point-blank range.

of time to pick the shot and take it from a good shooting position, cartridges like the .270 and .30-06 will do quite well, with bullets preferably being of 150 grains in the .270 and 180-200 grains in the .'06. The shot can be placed in the shoulder or lungs, and even if the bear lives a short time, he is not likely to get out of sight or reach the hunter to even the score. In these cases, it is best not to try to get too close, and anyone who shoots at a grizzly at over 200 yards is not using good judgement, unless it has been wounded.

These cartridges will give excellent results on the largest American game animals with the right load, no matter what the hunting situation. From left: 7mm Remington Magnum 175 gr. Remington Core-Lokt; .300 Winchester Magnum, 200 gr. Nosler; .300 Weatherby 180 gr. factory load; .338 Winchester Magnum 250 gr. Silver Tip factory load; .340 Weatherby 210 gr. Nosler; .375 H&H 300 gr. Silver Tip factory load.

If the grizzly is near the brush, rocks or other cover, or if you happen to bump into him at under 50 yards, the best plan is to break up as much bone as possible to immobilize him. A bullet through both shoulders will seldom kill quickly because it is forward of the lungs, but if you break one or both, he isn't likely to get to you before you can finish him off, or make it out of sight if he goes the other way. A quartering shot into the shoulder that goes on into the lungs, or through the lungs and into the off shoulder, is a quick killer, and slows the bear down at the same time. A spine/shoulder shot is the surest of all, but risky because the grizzly hump is conducive to high bullet placement because the spine appears to be higher than it actually is. A bear hit too high will go down, but he won't stay there.

Even though a mountain grizzly isn't especially big as compared to a bull moose, 500-600 pounds being a big one, it should be obvious that it will take a lot of penetration to break up his shoulders and go on inside. And if you want to put him down and keep him there, the bullet should pack a lot of punch and tear up a lot of bear meat.

Anything that applies to mountain grizzlies also applies to Alaskan brown bears, except that the brownie is a lot bigger than his inland relative, and it takes a lot more penetration and force to put him down. While I've killed a number of mountain grizzlies with 7mm and .30 magnums, and I once saw a small brownie knocked off with a 175-grain Nosler from a 7mm Remington Magnum with no problem, I feel a lot better with a .338, .340 or a .375 for most brown bear hunting. In the fall, most brownies are shot along the salmon streams, which means heavy brush in most areas, and often uncomfortably close ranges. And if you hunt them in the spring in Southeast coastal areas, most of the beaches are narrow, and they are only a few jumps from the solid wall of the rain forest. If you want that bear's hide, you had better break up one or both shoulders and/or the spine. For this it takes large caliber bullets of controlled expansion design, and if they are moving along at high velocity, it is even better.

I once hunted with an Alaskan brown bear guide who used a .450 Watts Magnum exclusively, part of the reason being that it served as a back-up gun if the hunter did a sloppy job and the bear got into the brush. That may be a bit more cartridge than is needed for general brown bear hunting, but maybe it's better to be on the heavy side than the light. In fact, I'd rather have a little too much gun than too little for any kind of game or hunting, just in case everything doesn't go quite right.

Rifle Actions for American Hunting

John Wootters

I sometimes believe that gun writers, myself included, have developed the art of hair-splitting to the ultimate degree. We'll pontificate for 3000 words on the subtle differences between the .270 WCF and the .280 Remington, for example, when the simple truth is that, for practical hunting purposes, there *is* no difference. None. Zilch. Zero. You can take a loaded specimen of either into the field, without knowing which, and slay a mule deer with it, and no human could say which cartridge did the work, from either the shooter's or the shootee's reactions.

Likewise, gallons of printer's ink are expended annually in learned analyses of rifle actions, comparing largely imaginary distinctions in accuracy, speed, or reliability. In the last paragraph of the treatise, we usually have a neatly-phrased, wrap-it-all-up statement of *the author's* preference. I promise solemnly that there will be no such ending here, because I'll state my own preferences going in. I *prefer* the looks, feel, and handiness of lever-action carbines, and I'm greatly taken with the whole aura surrounding the modern falling-block, single-shot hunting rifles . . . but I find myself toting a good bolt action about 97 percent of the time I can spend seriously in search of a big-game trophy. So be it; that's the difference between prejudice and practicality.

Obviously, neither my prejudices nor my perception of practicality are wholly shared by the balance of American hunters, since all four major types of rifle actions—five, counting the new/old single-shots—have enjoyed a brisk enough sale for a generation or two to keep them on the market. I'm no marketing expert, but I do know that you can't sell guns the way you sell toothpaste or laundry detergent, trying to convince the buyer to "try a tube and compare." A hunting rifle is a serious and long-term purchase. Gimmicks and radical innovations, no matter how meritorious, simply do not sell in the hunters' gun market, and what does not sell does not continue to be offered. Bolt actions, levers, slide actions and semiautomatics have all been around, on the average, for more than three quarters of a century, and that means that they *work*.

It does not necessarily mean that all of them work equally well for all types of hunting, however. The choice of an action can be dictated by a tremendous range of factors, from esoterica such as "it was good enough for Grandad and it's good enough for me" to a steely-eyed evaluation of the ballistic potentials of the available chamberings. Probably the only thing that keeps the slide-action rifles on the market today (and there are only two of them) is the fact that there are a lot of quail and duck hunters out there who cut their teeth on and still use pump shotguns. These fellows believe, rightly or otherwise, that they will be more effective in the field if their rifles and shotguns have the same type of mechanism. And, the power of sheer *belief* being what it is, they're most likely right; in any case, that's a perfectly legitimate reason for selecting a rifle action.

Ballistic potential is an important ingredient in such selections. I'm absolutely convinced that the right way to go about choosing a big-game rifle is to choose the right cartridge, and then go looking for a rifle in which to fire it. The cartridge is, after all, what does the work, while the rifle directs it safely and, hopefully, accurately. The most magnificent rifle ever made, chambered to the .22 Hornet, is all but useless in an encounter with an irate grizzly, whereas a cobby, plain .338 Magnum would be welcome in the same encounter, as long as it functioned. The difference lies in the cartridges, and not in the physical characteristics of the rifles. Similarly, the difference between the right rifle for whitetails in Michigan's cedar swamps and for whitetails in the Texas brush country, where shots run from long to longer, is in the cartridges. The .35 Remington may be fine for Michigan, but it's a total loss in most of south Texas, unless you figure on hitting your buck on the bullet's fourth or fifth bounce! That's why I say choose performance (which means the cartridge) first, and then pick the rifle model you like best that chambers that cartridge.

This is not as limiting as it used to be. For many years, the

Modern semiautomatics—from top, Browning BAR, Remington M742, and Ruger Carbine—are chambered to effective big-game cartridges, and offer considerably more accuracy, on the average, than they are often given credit for.

bolt action was your only choice (among modern rifles) if you wanted the ballistic performance of, say, the .30-06 and up. No semiautos, lever jobs, or pumps had been so chambered since the old Model 1895 Winchester, which was discontinued in 1936. But things have changed. You still can't buy a .30-06 lever action, but this chambering is available now in a pump, a couple of autoloaders and, of course, almost every bolt-action model manufactured. It's true that the selection of any *specific* cartridge may limit your choice of rifles to one (.300 Savage in the Model 99 Savage, .257 Roberts in the M77 Ruger, .35 Remington in the Merlin 336 or Mossberg 472, etc.), but you can usually find a rifle of your choice of actions to handle any general *category* of cartridge performance. The exception is the category of elephant cartridges; few American hunters have even an imagined need for such whale-wallopers as the .375 H&H or .458 Winchester Magnum, but those who do are stuck with bolt actions or single shots, among American products.

The oldest (and most traditionally American) repeating rifle action is, of course, the lever. Until sometime after the end of World War II, it was *the* standard "deer rifle." A Savage Model 99 was my first weapon for whitetails, back in 1940, when the majority of Texas hunters toted either an M99 or a Winchester Model 94. Most hunters of my generation grew up thinking "lever" whenever someone mentioned "deer," and there are enough of us still around to account for much of the lever action's popularity.

Nobody told us, in those days, that the typical lever-actioned rifle was apt to be chambered for a relatively mild cartridge, or that locking systems were on the weak side and extraction far below par. Nor were we much concerned with the inability of these carbines to shoot minute-of-angle groups, or the awkwardness of scoping most of them. We racked up some pretty good scores on whitetails with conventional iron or peep sights and thought nothing of it.

As a *group,* today's lever-actioned rifles still suffer all those

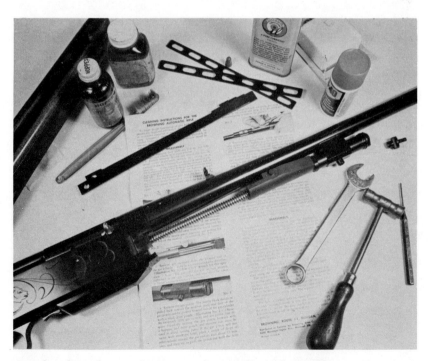

Autoloaders do require more thorough and regular maintenance than manual repeaters to insure functional reliability, and the cleaning procedures are more complicated and require more tools.

disadvantages, if indeed that's what they are, but various models available often avoid them. The Browning BLR, the Marlins and the Savage are eminently scopable. The Browning sports a front-locking, rotating-head locking system as strong as any, and it and the Savage are chambered to such high-intensity cartridges as the .308 and .243. The BLR and M99 are quite capable of excellent accuracy, really comparable to that of most run-of-the-mill bolt guns of comparable weight. All but the Savage have exposed hammers, a very positive safety system that many hunters like, myself included.

As a whole, the lever jobs do suffer somewhat in the extraction-power department, but this is mostly a problem for hand loaders. And hand loaders run into other problems with levers (stretched cases, for one) and seldom use them for serious hunting of big game these days.

On the plus side, today's lever-action guns are light, short, easy to carry and quick to point, and these are important considerations, especially for a deer hunter. They're mostly flat and handy for lugging in a saddle scabbard, and they're rugged and reliable if fed proper ammunition. As for speed of follow-up fire, the levers are second to none, not even the vaunted "automatics," if we're talking about *aimed* fire that hits the target. I regard the rapid-fire capabilities of any hunting rifle as an overrated and over-discussed matter, since the first shot is invariably the best shot you'll have at game. If it doesn't do the job, your odds on subsequent shots drop dramatically, and that's not the fault of the rifle.

This photo of the new Shilen DGA sporting-rifle action reveals the classic simplicity of the bolt-action type—simplicity that contributes to strength, reliability, accuracy and light weight.

Wootters' favorite rifle for medium-sized big game is this tried-and-proven bolt-action Sako Mannlicher in .308 WCF. Handy, light and quick, it has killed every animal at which it has ever been fired.

I can't resist mentioning one lever-action rifle that is no longer on the market, the Winchester Model 88. It was probably the most consistently accurate of its breed, and unquestionably the strongest and most modern design. I used one for 10 years and bitterly regret getting talked out of it, especially since this Winchester apparently couldn't compete in the marketplace with its stablemate, the M94, and died a premature death. It wasn't perfect, but it was as close as a lever-action designer has yet come.

In the 1950's, we had a horde of ex-GIs flooding the woods, many of whom had had their first and only experience with large-bore rifles in the military. There they had been trained with semiautomatics, and taught the "virtues" of target-saturation fire. They found they liked shooting, and came home looking for a sporting rifle with which they felt comfortable. Over the next decade or so, these fellows demanded and got autoloaders from Remington, Browning, Harrington & Richardson, Winchester and Ruger, and some writers predicted that the semiauto was about to drive all other types of actions off the market. Said scribes were wrong, I'm glad to report, but all those listed, ex-

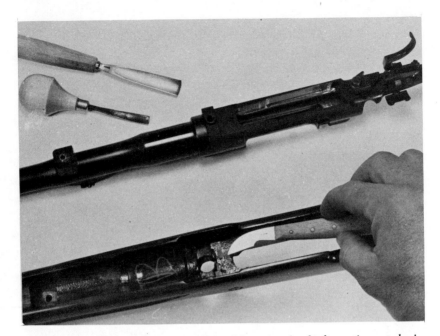

Fine-tuning the steel-to-wood bedding in the bolt-action style is less complicated, and the techniques are more standard, than with any other action—another reason for its popularity among serious riflemen/hunters.

cept the Winchester M100, are still to be found in the gunshops, and are selling well enough to keep the cash registers ringing.

The glamor seems to have faded from the quick-shooters, however, as the more serious types among the ex-soldiers discovered that volume-of-fire, fill-the-air-with-lead tactics don't work very well in the hunting field. What counts there is the well-aimed single bullet; we're not trying to keep a bull elk's head down while we assault his bunker, we're trying to kill him, as cleanly and humanely as possible.

Verily, this can be accomplished just about as well with an autoloader as any other kind of rifle, but *not* because it stokes itself without manipulation by the shooter. The only real advantage of the type is that the average hunter doesn't have to practice working the action in order to do it efficiently. I daresay I can hit a given target as often within a specified time limit with a bolt action as most men can with any self-shucker ever made, because long years of practice have taught me to jack the bolt about as quickly as I can recover from recoil and get the sights

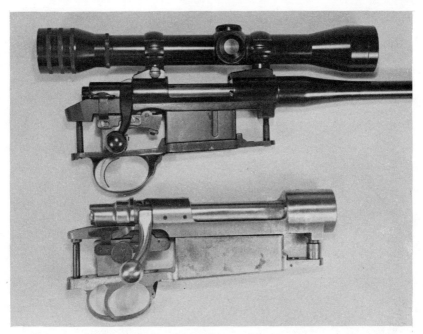

Bolt actions come in a variety of lengths, so that a rifle can be adapted to its cartridge without excess weight or bolt-travel. Here, the tiny Sako L461 action (for .222-class cartridges) is compared to a commercial FN Mauser action sized for .30-06- length rounds.

back in line. And the man with the auto also has to control recoil and realign his sights if he intends to hit anything. It's just that not even a subconscious part of his attention need be diverted from the target to reload his piece; the gas-operated action does it for him.

However, not even the most fanatic autoloader fan can deny that these actions are inherently more prone to what the military calls "stoppages," and are considerably more demand- ing of meticulous maintenance than any of the manually operated repeaters. Each step of the operating cycle is depen- dent upon the successful completion of the one preceding it, and that means that a faulty primer, a twig in the bolt raceways, a half teaspoonful of sand, or any of a hundred other impediments can bring the action to a sudden halt. It *may* be cleared by merely yanking on the operating handle, or it may not; usually not, in my observation. This is not to say that nothing can stop a bolt, lever or pump from shooting, but with these, a normal cycling of the action usually seems to clear it. Furthermore, the

The author prefers the bolt action for most game shooting. Here he poses with an African sable bull taken with a Browning Safari Grade .375 H&H Magnum. Note the clean neck shot.

force applied to a manual repeater's mechanism can be varied by the operator to meet the problem, whereas an autoloader's cycling is a fairly delicate balance of consistent forces.

If you wish to quibble with the comment about maintenance, I suggest you read the instruction booklets packed by Remington, Ruger, Browning, et al. with their self-stoking sporters; you'll find great emphasis on rather elaborate cleaning procedures, and, in the case of Remington, a special little brush designed for cleaning the chamber.

A quick check of the various reloading manuals also reveals that the quick-bangers also call for special care and attention in reloading, since gas-port pressures must fall within a certain fairly narrow range to insure reliable functioning with no battering of parts. For the most part, top loads for autos run a couple of grains of powder below those for bolt actions, since the autos share the problem of extraction power with the levers (and, for that matter, the slide actions).

It has been fashionable for quite some time to knock the accuracy potential of the self loaders, but I suspect that some of the writers who do the knocking haven't seriously target-tested many of the current crop. I have tested many, and I must admit that I was astonished at the grouping potential shown, especially by the Remington and Browning autos. I'm confident that these two models will *consistently* group as well at 100 yards from a bench-rest as will any of today's bolt-actioned sporters in the same chamberings, out of their respective boxes. I hear a few snickers and snorts, but don't call your bookie until you've shot a half-dozen or so of each model from a rest.

The gas guns do one thing, too, that no other kind of action can do, and that is reduce recoil sensation. This becomes important, especially in the Browning which is chambered for several big, belted magnums (.300 Winchester, .338 Winchester, etc.) which develop enough clout at the butt to give most shooters pause. The principle is exactly the same in these rifles as in gas-operated autoloading shotguns, and you can ask any skeet or trap-shooter about the benefits of softened recoil in those smoothbores.

On the whole, the semiautomatic rifles tend to be heavy, a bit bulgy and slab-sided, and quite long overall. The little Ruger

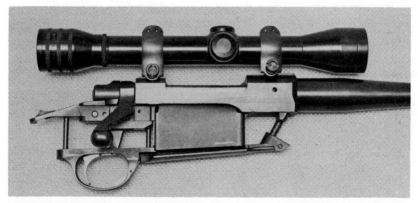

Almost all modern bolt actions are merely modifications of the original Mauser M98 design, but many—like this Ruger M77 with its angled front guard screw—incorporate minor, but significant, improvements.

The secret to rapid fire with a bolt action is technique and lots of practice. The bolt handle must never be grasped, nor the rifle lowered from the shoulder. In the first step (top) the bolt handle is slapped upward with the open palm.

Above
Now roll the palm toward your face and yank the bolt handle back with the little finger.

Opposite, above
The operating hand is now rotated to catch the bolt handle in the crook of the thumb, driving the bolt forward.

Opposite, center
Now the open hand slaps the bolt handle downward into the locked position.

Opposite, below
This movement automatically positions the hand on trigger and grip for the next shot. With practice, this sequence can easily be performed while the shooter recovers from recoil and brings the sights back on target.

60

The workings of the classic Savage Model 99 lever action are shown here. Remarkably "modern" when introduced at the turn of the century, this design still is hammerless, easily scopable, with side ejection, and strong enough for modern cartridges.

carbine is the exception, but it's offered only in the .44 Magnum chambering (a pistol cartridge, really). The rest of them are anything but trim and compact, and perhaps that's my principle objection to them. Above all else, a hunting rifle must carry and handle well, and the autos don't, at least for me. As for their reliability, I regard it as a drawback, but not much of one for any rifleman who maintains his weapons religiously, regardless of their type.

We come now to the slide-actions or "pumps," and there are only two on the market today, one from Remington and the other from Savage. The former comes in several modern cartridges, including the .270, .243, 6mm Rem., .308, .30-06 and others; the latter can be purchased only in .30-30. As mentioned before, their chief appeal seems to be to shotgunners who favor the same action style in a scattergun. Generally, they suffer the same problems as the others mentioned so far—weak extraction, something less than gilt-edged accuracy and the handling qualities of a fence-post. They are, however, more reliable than the autoloaders, just as fast in rapid fire (or faster) than lever actions, and they can be scoped, if you wish.

I have a special fondness for pumps, I must admit, because I shot my first whitetail with an old Remington Model 141 .35 Remington that I still own. It is one of the slickest, most beautifully-made rifles in my rack—but I've long since retired it in favor of more efficient hunting arms. I suspect the American hunter will likewise retire the entire class of actions, for the same reasons, within the foreseeable future. Too many young-sters are learning to shoot with autoloading shotguns to provide the deep reservoir of goodwill toward slide actions which has kept the pump rifles available until now.

The bolt-action rifle is a classic example of the truth in the saying that *class will tell*. Militarily, the bolt gun was finished by about the middle of World War II, 30 years ago, but as a sporting arm, this type was just getting started by then. Today, no major manufacturer of center-fire sporting rifles (except Mar-lin) considers his product line complete without a competitive bolt action, and the bolt gun is usually the very backbone of that line. This is just as true of English and European manufacturers as American firms, and the battle for market supremacy, as far as rifles are concerned, rages around the Winchester Model 70, the Remington Model 700, the Savage 110 and offspring, the Ruger M77, the Mossberg 810, and a host of Sakos, Husqvar-nas, BSA's, Finnish LSA's and Mausers, which speak every-thing from Belgian to Japanese, not to mention English with a South African accent! In short, the bolt-action rifle is slowly but steadily wiping out the competition. I have no contemporary sales statistics, but I'll risk a guess that more bolt-action center-fire rifles are sold every year in this country than specimens of all other action-types combined, and probably by a fairly wide margin. Joe Hunter may prefer a gas-operated shotgun or a lever

The ever-popular Winchester M94 carbine remains the all-time best seller among sporting rifles.

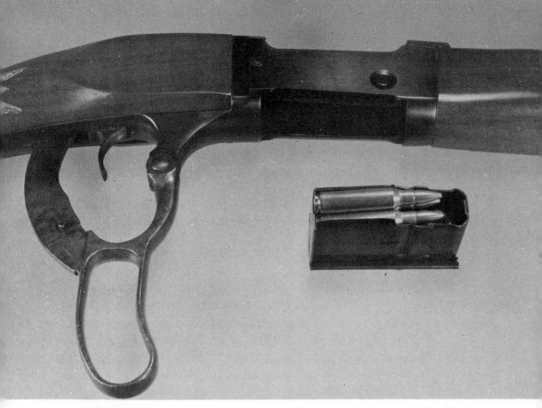

Of lever guns now in production, only this Savage Model 99 and the Browning BLR (not shown) are suited to modern, high-intensity cartridges (.308 WCF in this case) and detachable clip magazines.

This old .35 Model 141 Remington (no longer manufactured) shows the slide action in its natural habitat—thick woods where ranges are short and shots must be quick.

.22 rimfire, but he mostly wants a turnbolt with which to whack something in the javelina-to-brown-bear category, and even more so if his plans extend to Cape buffalo, elephant or the large African carnivores.

There are reasons. One is the aforementioned wide selection of models, manufacturers and price ranges. Another is the even wider selection of chamberings; just about every center-fire cartridge devised since the turn of the century is, or has been, chambered in somebody's bolt-action rifle, with the sole exception (that I can think of) of the .256 Winchester Magnum. Many of these cartridges have been available *only* in a bolt action, from the smallest (.17 Remington) to the largest (.460 Weatherby Magnum), so that a man who desired that particular performance level had no choice; it was a turnbolt or nothing. Some very good cartridges died on the vine, in fact, because

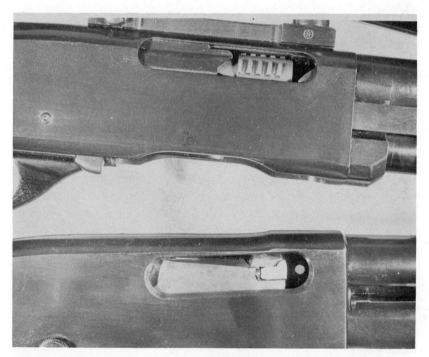

Mechanical improvements in modern Remington Model 760 slide action can be seen here, compared to the obsolete Remington M141 pump at bottom. Note the interrupted-thread locking lugs of the 760 that permit use of high-pressure cartridges such as the .243 and .270, and port for detachable box magazine, as opposed to the tubular style of older designs.

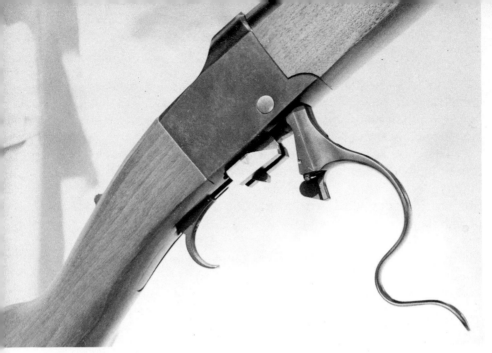

This close-up of the Ruger No. 3 falling-block, single-shot action reveals the compactness and simple operation of this particular gun.

they were *not* widely chambered in popular bolt-action models— among them the .280 Remington and .358 Winchester.

The bolt action has always enjoyed a good press. It has been called "the strongest, safest, most versatile, most reliable, and most accurate" of all sporter types. Overall, such high billing is probably justified, at least in the best examples of the type, although I have already mentioned that some other actions today challenge the bolt guns in several of those categories, and that all of them are strong *enough,* safe *enough,* and accurate *enough* for their intended purposes. The fact that most of the major writers on firearms and hunting topics for the last 30 years or so—Crossman, Page, O'Connor, Keith, Brown, Carmichel, and others—have used and written about bolt-action rifles almost to the exclusion of other types has probably influenced more consumers than all the technical advantages combined.

One of those advantages applies mainly to hand loaders who are wont to push their loads a bit in the pressure department. The bolt action is not only strong enough to hold the pressures, but the primary extraction cams are powerful enough to get over-pressured cases out of the chamber. Also, this simple, manually-operated mechanism lends itself to reduced loadings and non-standard bullet-seating depths, something to which most other actions do not take too kindly.

The Marlin Model 1895 lever action (below) and the Ruger No. 1 single-shot (above) are both chambered for the .45-70 Springfield cartridge. These strong rifles permit the old cartridge to be hand loaded to near-magnum ballistics.

As for accuracy, the run-of-the-mill turnbolt rifle may average slightly better than the typical lever or semiauto, but the difference is not as great as most hunters seem to believe. However, the bolt action's one-piece stock and simple, sturdy bedding system lends itself very readily to tinkering by the real accuracy buff, the necessary techniques being common knowledge and not beyond the ability of even a casual rifleman. Therefore, the bolt gun may or may not outshoot its competitors as it comes out of the box, but it can usually be made to do so without much trouble and without access to a machine shop.

Finally, the usual bolt-actioned sporter comes with a much better trigger than other types, and if the one furnished by the manufacturer cannot be adjusted to suit the particular shooter, it can be replaced by any of several custom trigger units that can. For the serious rifleman, this may be the single greatest advantage offered by bolt-operated rifles.

Perhaps that's the best description of the turnbolt action: It's the gun for the *serious* rifleman. He's the fellow who loads his own ammunition, is sensitive to trigger-action quality, is willing to tinker with bedding and won't settle for accuracy "good enough to hit a deer." He wants the best accuracy he can get, within the limits of his budget and the strength of his rifle-toting shoulder. He *always* scopes his weapon, and he fires enough practice rounds each year so that the bolt is no handicap to swift follow-up shots. However, he's much more concerned about spotting the first bullet where he wants it than his second and subsequent rounds.

The difference may be that the bolt action is the "rifleman's rifle," as Winchester used to advertise the Model 70, while the levers, pumps and autoloaders appeal more to the hunters to whom the rifle is nothing more than a utilitarian tool, who shoot factory ammunition, and who estimate accuracy by the carcasses hanging on the meatpole, rather than the size of the benchrest groups.

There was a day when the choice might be dictated by a hunter's left- or right-handedness, since the lever, pump, and autoloading actions are generally more suitable for use from either shoulder. However, in recent years, several of the most popular bolt models have been marketed in mirror-image, left-handed versions so that southpaws can no longer make any claim of discrimination.

The other type of rifle action which deserves discussion is not a magazine repeater, but is nonetheless a serious hunting weapon. It is the falling-block single shot, as exemplified by the Ruger No. 1 and No. 3, the Browning M78, the new Wickliffe, and others. Although functionally and in appearance they are throwbacks to the 1880's and the heyday of the great Winchesters, Sharps and other one shooters, the modern single-shots are really a 20th-century development, with coil springs, investment-cast parts and super-steel alloys. They are more sophisticated in every way than their ancestors and namesakes, and they're thoroughly practical hunting arms. Because they lack a magazine, they dispense with the typical long receiver required by a repeating action. This means that the single-shot can either be very compact and handy with a normal-length barrel or about the same length and weight as a bolt gun with a much longer barrel. Longer barrels, of course, offer better ballistics, especially with the popular smallbore magnum cartridges. A Ruger No. 1 with a 26-inch tube is a little shorter overall than a Remington M700 with a 22-inch barrel. In the same chambering, the turnbolt may give away as much as 200 feet per second to the falling-block, in return for the repeat-fire capability. Since I have already expressed my opinion on the value of repeat fire in the hunting field, no more need be said on that point.

For the hand loader, the single-shot offers even more flexibility than a bolt action, and some of them—the Rugers, in particular—are even stronger than the best bolt guns.

This is the author and his professional hunter in Mozambique, gloating over the great leopard taken in 1972 with the Ruger single-shot rifle shown, as described in the text.

A single-shot hunting rifle may not, in the eyes of the average hunter, be as "practical" all around as a sound repeater, and most of them cost more, so the proven sales appeal of the falling blocks has to be attributed to something else. That "something else" is, I believe, plain old snobbishness. A man who extracts a one-shot rifle from a case in a hunting camp seems to be saying something about his belief in his own shooting skill and his woodsmanship, and, perhaps, something about his concept of sportsmanship and hunting ethics. I have seen the effect of this silent statement on many fine hunter/riflemen when I uncased one of my own pet pair of Ruger No. 1's (a .30-06 for long-range work and a matched .45-70 for close-in brush-busting) . . . and I know for sure it has made some sales for one-shooter manufacturers.

Am I serious about really hunting with the single-shots? Judge for yourself: I selected that above-mentioned .45-70 for one of the most important shots I've ever fired at living game, a record-book African leopard in Mozambique in 1972. I'd traveled too far, waited too long and spent too much money to have that chance at my personal trophy-of-a-lifetime to choose any but the rifle I had the deepest confidence in, the best within reach for the purpose. The leopard never even heard that single cartridge explode; the big bullet snuffed him out too quickly.

Sure, I could probably have nailed him just as efficiently with any of several other rifles we had along on that safari, but the No. 1 was the one I *wanted* to use, the one I was most comfortable with in those circumstances. That feeling is a powerful reason for choosing and using any rifle, of whatever action type or whatever chambering, for the game you have in mind at the moment.

No technical advantage, no split hairs over split-second operation, no engineering jargon laced with decimal points, coefficients and PSI's can possibly be more important in the field than this sensation of confidence, comfort and liking the feel of a rifle. If you have it for your rifle, *never* let anyone talk you out of it. That relationship between a hunter and his arm is priceless.

If you don't have it, or if you're just easing into this big-game hunting business, buy a good bolt-action sporter, mount a good scope, and begin now to get yourself on intimate terms with it.

Chances are, you'll never change.

Rifle Accuracy

Jac Weller

Every rifleman in the world wants a delivery system that can kill anything from rabbits to moose with a single bullet at any range from 10 to 1000 yards, and score V's every time on targets at all ranges. This straight-shooting all-purpose rifle has not been invented yet, and never will be. Most firearms shoot "straighter" than the hunters or competitors who use them. Actually, once a good bullet is in stable flight, it travels in a straight line, excepting allowances for wind and gravity. Accuracy for a given rifle depends on firing successive bullets in the same relation to the point of aim. For the time being, let's forget about the most important factor influencing this regularity, the fellow pulling the trigger.

All hunting rifles must be zeroed so the bullets land on point of aim or slightly above at 100 yards. There is no point in worrying about the ability of your bullet delivery system to issue successive bullets properly until you have an acceptable zero, which may not remain constant for more than a few weeks. Imperfect zeros account for more disappointments than any other mechanical detail.

Once you are sure you can place the center of your group on point of aim, the capability of your rifle to shoot small groups at all practical ranges is important. If your rifle won't group well on a target, you may be seriously handicapping yourself in the field. About 400 years ago, spiral grooves were put inside the barrels of firearms to make them into rifles. Bullets that spin about the axis of their flight do tend to strike closer to the point of aim than those that tumble, although not all rifles are equally accurate. As I write, I have in front of me a target with five 7.62 bullets fired at 100 yards in .30 inches. Another group of similar bullets fired in the same manner has an extreme spread of more than 8 inches. These two groups represent about the best and the worst we are likely to encounter in modern hunting rifles.

Let's get one thing straight at the start. There is more to a hunting arm than the ability to fire small groups. You just cannot take the ultimate accuracy of bench-rest rifles with you into the field, because powerful telescopic sights are not portable. Even if you were strong enough to carry one of these beasts and remain fresh enough to shoot it, how could you get into action quickly in a scrub oak thicket or semi-swamp? Reloading a single-shot bench-rest rifle—they are all single-shot—takes several seconds. Compromise in accuracy, portability, and easy handling must be made, and will depend upon your game and where you hunt.

A woodchuck shooter in open country, especially if he has a jeep or pick-up truck, can use a heavy delicate rifle. If he is a good shot, a good judge of range, and his chosen his "stand" well, he will succeed in spite of a heavy, awkward rifle. But even "light varmiter" category bench-rest rifles are too heavy for most of us to carry far, and too clumsy to get into action quickly. When I was younger, I did use heavy, powerful rifles in Wyoming and Alaska, but settled for something lighter, handier and more quickly reloadable along the Eastern Seaboard from Maine to Georgia.

Another reason you may choose a bullet delivery sytem that gives less than maximum accuracy is that cartridges used with bench-resters are never magnums. Maybe you will want more power or flatter trajectory than you can get with ammunition that gives the tightest groups at 100 and 200 yards.

With the above in mind, let's see if we can break down sporting rifles into categories according to use in the field. More center-fire arms are bought and used by Americans in the hunting of Eastern whitetail deer than for all other classes of big game combined. These animals are seldom shot at ranges greater than about 100 yards, and most at less than half that. Whitetail deer are fairly large targets, and are not hard to kill, Power requirements are surely not greater than the .30-06, if that high.

On the other hand, this hunting can be strenuous and the country thick. Light, fast-handling rifles are desirable, even if they entail some sacrifice of accuracy. The most inaccurate, ac-

An unfired-on CFC Rocky Mountain Sheep target. Outside diameter of the 'plus rings' in the heart area is 3½", but these cannot be seen through the highest-power scopes allowed (4X).

ceptable American rifle, if properly zeroed, will kill a standing buck at 100 yards if the bullet is directed properly. Let's call this "category one accuracy."

The second category will be rifles normally used by chuck hunters. As mentioned, it is possible to use bench-rest rifles for this, so accuracy is of top importance. Any good bullet will do, but it should travel fast for flat trajectory, which minimizes the need for range corrections.

"Category three accuracy" is needed by hunters who go after moose and brown bear in Alaska, elk in Wyoming, and antelope in Texas. Rifles used for this hunting should give as close to "category two accuracy" as possible, but they must be portable. There are also problems of bullet power and effectiveness on a big target. For instance, a bullet that will kill a woodchuck

Weller and the winning rifle, a Remington Model 40X in 6mm Remington with 24-inch barrel. The whole rig was reduced to a gross weight of 11.0 pounds, including the scope.

quickly may not be powerful enough to handle an 1100-pound bull elk, and wouldn't be safe for Kodiak bear. Regardless of caliber, however, you want all the accuracy you can carry to and through the area where you will hunt. In the West and in Alaska, ranges can be at least as long as those encountered in woodchuck sport, but game is bigger. The 7mm Remington Magnum, 7.62 NATO, and .30-06 may be about as low as some of us would like to go for elk and bear, although small deer and antelope can probably be killed satisfactorily with most center-fire rifle cartridges. Remember, however, that all bullets lose energy with range. Make sure the one you choose is still adequate to the maximum range at which you are likely to fire. Energy plus proper placement and bullet type lead to successful kills.

What about really dangerous game? In America, grizzly and

brown bears are about all we have. Any rifle carried by a hunter who goes after these two bears should have enough power and maneuverability to handle them at close range. In a crisis, like stopping a wounded bear, only "category one accuracy" is required, but you need all the power possible.

Brown bear hunting in Alaska is not limited to shots at close range. Some fine animals have been killed beyond 300 yards. You may need "category three accuracy," or as much of it as you can retain with the required power.

I have not hunted at all in Africa, and only twice briefly in South Asia. I understand, however, that dangerous thin-skinned game is frequently killed at moderately long range, say around 200 yards. I am told that since hunters now seldom carry two rifles with them at the same time, they need both power and accuracy in the same arm, like the rifles mentioned above for brown bear. Fine American-made hunting rifles of the "Safari" type give you both, but most hunting delivery systems chambered for the .458 Winchester Magnum cartridge kick infernally. The only ways to prevent this are to increase the rifle weight and to add an oversize recoil pad. None of us notices recoil when actually firing at game, but one must get to know his rifle beforehand. Recoil, and the instinctive fear of it, can spoil carefully learned habits of trigger control.

I had Roy Weatherby make me a special heavy rifle—it weighed 13 pounds 1 ounce—in his .460 Magnum caliber, and I shot a brown bear on Kodiak Island with it at a range exceeding 300 yards. I also won a club accuracy competition with this same rifle that will be described presently. Big powerful calibers can be accurate if the rifle isn't too heavy, but I'm not sure how practical something of this sort is in America. This rifle is near ideal for all dangerous game at any range, anywhere, *if* you can carry it. I can't anymore, and don't recommend it to anyone of average strength, even if he is young and in near-perfect physical condition. You can get, of course, a rifle chambered for the .460 Weatherby Magnum cartridge that weighs less than ten pounds, but it will recoil so badly that you can't do the necessary practice for satisfactory accuracy in the field.

Summarizing briefly, "category one accuracy" is sufficient for game at ranges where these animals become dangerous. Since far more are shot at moderate distances than close, you may want as much of "category three accuracy" as you can retain. But don't handicap yourself for close shooting just to have another 50 yards of effectiveness where it isn't vital.

Metallic Silhouette Competition

Until fairly recently, most competitive target shooting with rifles in the United States was of the Camp Perry type. I am excluding for the moment the bench-resters. Big-bore rifles used at Perry events, except for the Wimbledon, have iron sights. Since most experienced hunters now use scopes on their rifles, the correlation between target shooting and hunting is loose. Hundreds of thousands of American hunters have never even seen a National Match course range nor fired a rifle suitable for use on one. Competitive shooters do go hunting; hunters do compete on targets. But the two sports are quite different.

About 20 years ago, a new target rifle sport began in Mexico and has now spread through most of this country. Contestants shoot at black steel silhouettes at ranges to 500 meters with scope-sighted rifles of limited weight. These bullet delivery systems must be capable of knocking down over 50-pound steel plates as far as 547 yards away. Even the .25-06 is only successful once out of three average hits. These MS (metallic silhouette) shooters use no special gloves or clothing, nor any non-hunting equipment. Slings, thumb-hole stocks, palm rests and similar contrivances are all barred. All legal rifles must have functioning magazines.

After I accepted the assignment to write this chapter, I decided to compete in one of these matches. I learned a lot from talking to and watching veterans of MS shooting, which closely approximates hunting in Wyoming, Alaska and Scotland. These men shoot standing with ten-pound-three-ounce scope-sighted rifles at armor-plate targets that are 200, 300, 385 and 500 meters away. These targets are shaped like chickens, pigs, turkeys and desert sheep, five of them for each competitor at each range. You are allowed to use more than one rifle in most MS matches —one for each range if you like—but this probably isn't practical. You can also use iron sights if you prefer, but most competitors don't. The winners use just one rifle, but adjust their sights for each range. These metallic targets are roughly equal to V's over the National Match course with wind doping often necessary at 385 and 500 meters. I failed to knock over a single of the ten shot at 500 meters, but still pass on what I saw and heard.

First, these competitors prefer to use bolt-action rifles almost exclusively.

Second, the better shooters had fixed-power telescopic sights with a magnification greater than most hunters normally

Another view of the previously shown rifle and its winning target that scored a 150 + 60.

take into the field, but with positive adjustments for both range and windage.

Third, in the order of preference, calibers were 7.62 NATO (.308 Winchester), .30-06, and .280 Remington. These are the most powerful long-range cartridges available, since most range rules prohibit magnums that will destroy quickly the 200- and 300-meter targets.

Fourth, bullets used by successful competitors are all virtually of a single type, hollow-point for accuracy and boat-tailed in order to sustain velocity. Most weigh 168-200 grains and are hand loaded to or near maximum velocities. A few men use lighter bullets for the closer ranges.

MS shooting is, of course, extremely specialized. Not many of us will ever take a shot at a game animal as far away as 547 yards. Even if we did, we would probably contrive to use some position more stable than off-hand. The great virtue of this competition is that each shot is immediately a visible hit or miss; there is nothing in between. Further, there is no pit detail. Four young people mounted on motorcycles put back all knocked over targets at all four ranges in less than five minutes.

This shooting sport is practical, fast moving and fun. Skill is rewarded, but not to the exclusion of luck. A turkey hit in the foot is 'dead,' although a bullet closer to your aiming point can be a miss. The rules were made so as to allow only real hunting rifles. What these dedicated shooters have found out is certainly worth observing, but a flat-shooting rifle with a 20-power externally-adjusted scope wouldn't be needed for hunting Eastern whitetail deer, nor would it go efficiently into a saddle rifle scabbard in Wyoming. Some MS rifles have two ounce triggers.

Basis of Accuracy

Hunting rifle accuracy is not an attribute of the rifle alone—but of the rifle, the ammunition and the hunter. If any one of the three is defective, the combination will probably not work successfully in the field. As already indicated, the hunter himself is the most likely of the three to fail. Absolutely none of us was worth much when we began; game experience and lots of practice at targets (including dry firing) are required. But this chapter is devoted to the rifle and ammunition only. Ammunition is simpler, so let's deal with it first.

Factory-loaded rounds in some calibers still don't give the accuracy of which some rifles are capable. All bench-rest shooters and most dedicated chuck-hunters load their own. I hand load for competition and for indoor firing with hunting rifles, but I have taken most of my modest string of trophies, plus a lot of whitetail deer, with factory ammo which is, in some calibers, as good as most of us produce.

Recently I wanted some once-fired 6mm Remington cases and put a box of store-bought rounds through my favorite rifle in this caliber. Much to my surprise, I shot 13 X's out of 15 shots at 100 yards on a standard 100-yard small-bore target prone with sling using 80-grain factory bullets. This is as good as I can do with any hand-loaded combination, or ever could. No hunter need feel handicapped with ammunition loaded by one of the leading American firms, especially in the calibers where gilt-edged accuracy is likely to be required.

It is important when choosing ammunition to get a bullet that will do its job. You don't want the animal to run for a considerable distance, even though hit hard in a vital place. Generally, a heavier, less expandable bullet will accomplish this better than a light hollow-point, even though the latter is flatter shoot-

Weller in firing position with his 39-year-old sporter made from a World War I U.S. Model 1917 Enfield.

ing. It's sometimes possible to increase velocity with even a heavy bullet to improve trajectory, but this can lead to unpleasant recoil in rifles that are light enough to be carried easily in the hunting field. If you must hand load your hunting cartridges, fire some of them before you go, not only to recheck your rifle's zero, but to make sure the fired cases extract easily. A stuck cartridge due to too much pressure is nearly impossible to remove without tools.

On the other hand, if you do like to shoot and have some sort of range available, but are not rich, you will hand load for practice and pleasure. Primers, powder and even fine competition bullets cost only a fraction of what factory ammunition does today. Bench-resters continue to improve their groups towards five bullets through the same caliber diameter hole, all hand loads.

Personally, I like to shoot at 50 feet with the same rifle I'm going to shoot in the field or next time I go to an MS match. False chambers are disappointing, but you can load full-charge-fired, but only neck resized cases in most any caliber, so the de-

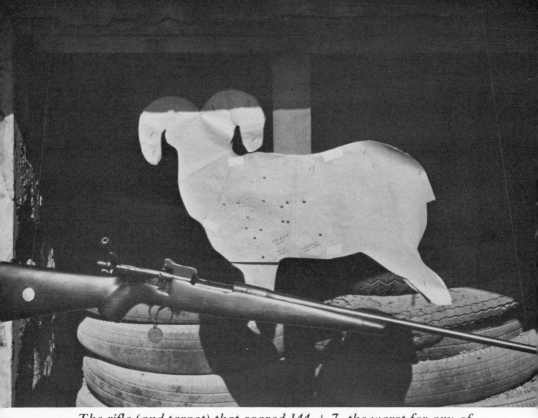

The rifle (and target) that scored 144 + 7, the worst for any of the fourteen rifles that completed the 15-round test. The rifle and Bishop sporter stock cost less than $10 total in 1938.

livery system is accurate, but no more powerful than a .45 ACP pistol. The more you practice, up to a point, the more accurate your own personal combination of hunter, ammunition and rifle will be.

Now let's consider your rifle. There are several design factors that are likely to lead to accuracy in rifles of the hunting type. First and foremost, the type of action. There are at least six available in American sporting goods stores today. All are satisfactory for some types of game under some circumstances, or they wouldn't still be on the market. I have already mentioned that MS shooters use bolt-action rifles almost exclusively; so do bench-resters. I read this sentence written by an expert recently: "Only bolt-action rifles produce top accuracy." Oh, yes? What about the superb U.S. National Match M1's and M14's after they have been worked on by the riflesmiths of Benning, Quantico and San Diego? What about our most recent sniper rifle, the XM21? But none of these is a hunting rifle, nor legal for game in some states.

Even though bolt-action delivery systems are, as a class, more accurate than the others, not every bolt-action hunting rifle is necessarily more accurate than individual specimens of the other types. Other actions, including both pumps and those reloaded by operating a lever, can be made to shoot well. The Ruger Rifle Number 1—a modified Ferguson single shot—has done extremely well recently in at least one caliber. All these have advantages over the bolt-action types, especially in regard to total length and handiness. Some will deliver a second shot quicker and more easily, especially for young men not trained in dummy round rapid-fire drill with the old '03 Springfield.

Let's pursue this design question a little further. If bolt-action arms are more accurate—they are generally a little cheaper to produce as well—why are the others still manufactured? The bolt-action design is longer and heavier than all its competitors with similar specifications. Many Eastern deer hunters prefer a type of arm that is easier to carry, more handy in thick cover, and quick to reload. They want only a medium heavy bullet traveling at moderate velocity, so they don't need extra weight just to absorb recoil. A pump, lever action or even a semiautomatic gives some men more confidence than a bolt gun for hunting. Sure, accuracy suffers slightly in most cases, but at short range, the loss isn't meaningful. A quick second shot is more to be desired.

On the other hand, hunters who go long distances in search of more prestigious game usually want to be able to pull off that long shot if they should get it, like an elk at 300 yards. A bolt action is best under those conditions, but not just any bolt action. You need a good one that will shoot tight groups for you.

The number-one reason for the superiority of bolt rifles to other types is that it is easier to fit the action to the stock for uniform bullet delivery round after round. Most bolt-action rifles now use a recoil shield or shoulder, a rectangle of steel solidly attached to the action that projects down into the stock. Modern rifles are not as smooth as the good ones before WW I, but they shoot better because of this feature: If the bedding at this point has been done properly, other inletting isn't necessarily precise. Disassemble your favorite. You will probably find that the wood in contact with the recoil shield is the only part of the stock that shows evidence of handwork.

What about the fit between barrel and fore-end? Ultimate accuracy bench-rest rifles have "free-floating" barrels, which means that the barrel does not touch the fore-end at all. A few hunting rifles are made in this manner at the factory, but not many. If in doubt about what you have, try passing an ordinary piece of writing paper down between barrel and stock. If it goes all the way back to the action, the barrel is "free floating."

It is not difficult to "free float" the barrels of most bolt-action sporting rifles, as long as you have enough wood in the stock to hold the action securely, but this may not be advisable. Just cutting away wood from under the barrel won't necessarily produce one minute of angle groups. The main argument against factory-produced free-floating barrel hunting rifles seems to be that the general public won't understand the "poor barrel fit" and think they have bought an inferior product.

Let's take Remington for example. All their Model 40X's are free floated because these arms are usually sold to target shooters, bench-resters and others who understand that the gap between barrel and fore-end is necessary for maximum accuracy, and has been produced in this manner intentionally. In my opinion, the reason the barrel of the Model 700 varmiter is not free floated is because it doesn't look good to some sportsmen. Remington spends more time and money getting light contact between metal and wood, especially in the area above the front sling swivel, than it would take to free float. This rifle shoots superbly well the way it leaves the factory, but can sometimes be improved by a little wood removal.

Free-floating barreled rifles require more careful fitting of their actions to their stocks, a process often referred to as bedding. I'm no expert at this, but have watched skilled mechanics rub blue on the action, tighten it down into the stock, remove it and then chisel out minute quantities of colored wood. Another method is to chisel out too much, replace with plastic fiberglass and let this set. At least two companies use heated actions for this fitting of the action to wood.

Another factor to be considered in choosing a particular hunting rifle is its reliability, including that of the sighting equipment you plan to attach to it. Common sense is important here. If you chuck-hunt in your own meadow, you can use a more delicate combination than if you are going above the snow line on Kodiak Island. It is better to have a simple sound mechanism, especially against dangerous game, than a more accurate, but more fragile delivery system. Hunters in Africa used side-by-side top-break double rifles shooting cartridges like the .557 and .600 Nitro Express for decades. Because of the present extreme cost of weapons of this type, and the difficulty of obtaining am-

Another view of Weller examining a bulls-eye target for zero before beginning to fire a test string.

munition (even components for reloading), these men have had to change, but most have chosen Mauser-type bolt-action rifles firing powerful cartridges that can be bought still, especially the .458 Winchester. Most of these men have, I believe, lighter bolt-action rifles equipped with scope sights, but when the chips are really down, they use powerful guns with iron sights.

It is hard for most of us to check up on bedding, and near impossible to evaluate details of rifling and accuracy factors, such as lock up between barrel and action and concentricity between bore and chamber. I'm told that a bolt that does not fit properly by a couple of thousandths of an inch can ruin an otherwise near-perfect combination. The possibility of minor mechanical defects in lever actions, pumps and semiautomatics is greater because there are more parts that must be properly fitted together for superior performance. Besides, there is less rigidity in most non-bolt-action basic designs; but we don't need to be expert rifle inspectors to determine accuracy. There is an easier, surer and cheaper way. Shoot your rifle five times at a target at about 100 yards from your own steadiest position. A solid shooting bench will help, but isn't necessary. The size of

The Remington Model 742 Woodsmaster in .308 Winchester that scored 150 + 18.

your group is the measure of the accuracy of your whole bullet delivery system, including you, your rifle and the ammunition you are firing.

With the above firmly in mind, I fired a selection of 15 different modern hunting rifles 15 shots each at 100 yards. I'm not a bench-rest shooter, and I prefer to fire prone. I normally use a sling, glove and rifle jacket. For comparison purposes, I used the Campfire Club Rocky Mountain sheep target, which is about 1/3 natural size. Groups fired at this target at 100 yards are roughly equal to shooting at 300 yards in the field. Again for comparison purposes, I used the CFC scoring system, ten points for a hit in the vital forward area, plus up to five additional points per shot for hits in the scoring rings centered in the heart area. The target is reproduced here to show how this scoring works. This sort of firing is more accurate than most hunters will achieve in the field, but is roughly comparable to it. Groups fired from a bench are not.

First, I fired my U.S. 1917 Enfield Sporter bought from the Director of Civilian Marksmanship in 1937. I installed the entire

The Winchester Model 88 lever action also chambered for the .308 Winchester cartridge that scored 150 + 31.

sighted and barreled action in a Bishop stock for a total cost of about ten dollars for everything. It still has its original iron sights and fires, of course the .30-06 cartridge. It is old, worn, long and crude, but has given me more pleasure than any other single firearm I have ever owned. Also, it is representative of tens of thousands of converted military rifles still being used in this country. I tightened up the stock screws and cleaned some grease from the bore. Its zero was fine vertically, but needed a correction of about eight minutes of angle horizontally. Since there is no simple and positive way of making this adjustment, I held off. Thirteen of my fifteen record rounds were in the chest cavity; the other two were just to the rear of it. My score of 144 + 7 turned out to be the lowest for any rifle fired, but holding off with old eyes and iron sights isn't recommended for precision shooting. There are surely, however, poorer hunting rifles still being used in the field today.

Second, I chose a Remington pump (Model 760 "Game-master") chambered for the 6mm Remington cartridge. This rifle is considered ideal by many Eastern whitetail deer hunters.

I was using a 2½ power scope, but no sling. I wasn't sure whether the fore-end, which is not attached to the barrel, would stand one. This rifle had an even further handicap for precise slow-fire target shooting because it had a shotgun-type release trigger, something that is disconcerting, to say the least. All fifteen bullets were in the chest cavity. Five were out of the plus points, but the worst shot was 3.4 inches away from dead center. The score was 150 + 27, with every round surely lethal on a real animal at 300 yards. Who said a well-designed slide-action rifle in a good caliber won't shoot?

Third, I tried a Winchester Model 88 lever action in .308 Winchester (7.62 NATO). Even though this model is lever-operated, it has (as Winchester claims) many bolt-rifle features. I had a 4X scope attached, a strong sling and a shotgun recoil pad to lengthen it for comfortable shooting. The score was 150 + 31, with only three rounds out of the plus points. I was using factory ammunition. Obviously, this combination is also lethal.

Fourth, I used an Ithaca Turkey Gun made in Finland with a 12-gauge shotgun barrel above, and a .222 Remington rifle barrel below. I fired only the rifle barrel in these tests, and scored a 150 + 22. The first five shots were all in the plus points, but the rifle barrel tended to "walk" with heat towards one o'clock after that. Surely good enough to kill a turkey, even at maximum yards.

Fifth, a Remington automatic (Model 742 Woodsmaster) in .308 Winchester (7.62 NATO). The score of 150 + 19 was about as expected. Most auto-loading rifles just don't have maximum accuracy, but the worst shot was only 3.75 inches from the center of the plus point rings.

Sixth, a Ruger Rifle No. 1 in .458 Winchester. I had installed a shotgun-type recoil pad, but the fine rifle was too much for me in prone position. It kicks unmercifully, so much that I gave up before the 15th shot the first time I tried to fire it for record. I began to miss the target about my fifth shot. The fault was mine, not the rifle's. I waited a week, and fired five shots for record. Total score 50 + 2. The accuracy is there, I truly believe, but I can't get it at 64 years old. I'm more worried about cutting my forehead than I should be. I believe this rifle would be at its best with iron sights at close range. It is short, stubby and gives confidence.

Seventh, a Winchester Model 70 Varmiter chambered for the .243 Winchester cartridge. The heavy barrel gives good stability; I expected to score higher than I did, a 150 + 34. I wasn't

The Remington Model 760 Gamemaster in 6 mm Remington. The target behind, scored 150 + 27, was fired with this rifle using a shotgun-type release trigger, but no sling. (A fine performance considering these handicaps.)

pleased with my holding, but fourteen shots were in the plus points. I pulled one round just out at nine o'clock.

Eighth, a Remington Model 700 Varmiter in a 6mm Remington. This rifle is standard except for the shotgun recoil pad, but it came from the factory several years ago with a free-floating barrel. The score was 150 + 48, with one bullet hole not in the plus rings. This flyer was probably my fault, although I wasn't conscious of a poor shot. I hand loaded this ammunition using new cases and bench-rest-type 70-grain bullets. This combination gets close to maximum accuracy for the position, target and firer.

Ninth, a Model 40X Remington in .257 Weatherby chambered by Roy Weatherby in his California shop. I dreamed up this bullet delivery system for maximum long-range accuracy before I hunted red deer in Scotland. It was at that time the flattest-shooting hunting rifle obtainable. I missed a shot—just over the deer's shoulder, according to the gamekeeper through a 30X telescope—at 500 yards. I took the same stag two hours later at 280 paces. This rifle is tops for something of this nature. Again, fourteen of the fifteen shots were in the plus points, with one just out, but the total was only 150 + 41. Mike Walker, who originally made the rifle and examined all my targets, said that I was pushing the bullets too fast for best accuracy, and that the lead cores were starting to melt. Some holes had grey stains around them. Weatherby rifles usually are free-bored, which can increase group size slightly, but they do have that small extra amount of trajectory flatness and/or power.

Tenth, a Remington Model 40X I used for hunting on several occasions. It was chambered originally for the 6 × 47 Remington, and won the Campfire Club sheep competition in that caliber on more than one occasion. When the Club changed its rules to disallow the 6 × 47, I had it rechambered for the 6mm Remington cartridge. At the same time, it lost three inches of barrel and enough wood—mostly in the form of holes drilled into the stock—to weigh precisely 11 pounds. I still have a 15-shot CFC sheep target fired with this rifle chambered for the 6 × 47 on 9 August 1972 that scores 150 + 60, the best I ever shot with any rifle until this last autumn. After Remington did the rechambering and cut off the barrel, I replaced the Buehler mounts and the Lyman 4X scope (the maximum power allowed in CFC rifle competition) on the barreled action, and re-attached the lightened stock. I fired the box of new Remington 6-mm ammunition mentioned earlier. The first shot was within 4 inches of the old zero; one sight adjustment, and I was dead center on the 100-yard small-bore target, with results already described.

Increasing cartridge size without any change in bore diameter is supposed to hurt accuracy, but I fired a 150 + 55 with this rifle—we call it the Paul Gogal after the fellow at Remington who supervised the rechambering—getting ready for the 1976 Fall Outing at the CFC. During the tests for this chapter, I shot another 150 + 60 tying my former best with any rifle. In other words, this particular rifle is as accurate now with its new larger powder-capacity cartridge as it was before, in spite of losing a couple of pounds in weight and three inches of barrel length. Younger men may fire higher scores, but this rifle is the best I have ever had. It looks funny now that it weighs only 11 pounds, complete with scope, but it will still shoot.

Eleventh, a Remington Model 40X in 7mm Remington Magnum. A similar rifle and cartridge won the Camp Perry Wimbledon at 1000 yards. It weighs 12 pounds and 1 ounce with scope, but for 15 shots prone plus sighters with 7mm Magnum recoil, you need the weight to save your shoulder. I used hand

Remington Model 700 Varminter in 6 mm Remington, and its target that scored 150 + 48.

loads with 160-grain Sierra Spitzer point boat-tail bullets in front of 60.3 grains of IMR 4350 in once-fired cases, and scored 150 + 52. No shot was worse than a plus 2. This combination had the second highest score fired, and may be the best in the world for hunting large game at long range. Sierra gives this bullet a "ballistic coefficient" of .561, second only in their entire handbook to their hollow-point Matchking of 168 grains in the same caliber. If it can win the Wimbledon at Perry for the Navy's Tom Treinen at 1000 yards, it will surely kill your big game for you, if you do your part.

Twelfth, a Ruger Model 77 in .220 Swift with a 26-inch medium-heavy barrel to take full advantage of the powder capacity of this powerful cartridge. After more than 40 years, it is still the only cartridge available with a factory loading to give more than 4000 foot/second muzzle velocity. My score of 150 + 38 was a disappointment because this combination will really shoot. But conditions were not good that day. A note on the target read, "Bright sun at 12:00 o'clock." I'm sure I could do better another time, but it wouldn't be fair to repeat for one and not for others. Every group of 15 shots was the first I fired for record —after sighting in on a bulls-eye target—except where clearly stated in regard to the Ruger .458 and the Paul Gogal. This cartridge (.220 Swift) still holds the all-time CFC sheep record fired by Jack Hessian of Winchester long ago; Mike Walker of Remington holds the new record since caliber was restricted to 6 mm and larger.

Thirteenth, another Remington Model 40X, this time in the old long-range favorite .300 H&H Magnum. I believed that the rifle was at least partially shot out. Several competitors, including myself, fired it for several years at Perry. Conditions were not ideal, but then the sun went under a cloud. My score was 150 + 51, the third best. I had one flyer out of the scoring rings at five o'clock, with a plus 1 at two o'clock, but the rest were 3's or better, well-centered.

Fourteenth: Save for my unsettling experience with the .458 Winchester cartridges in the Ruger Rifle Number One, I had fired only rifles with reasonably pleasant recoil. I was using heavy arms usually equipped with thick recoil pads. But now, I was in for some more shaking up. One rifle was an old Winchester Model 70 in .375 H&H Magnum that has gone to Alaska, Newfoundland and Wyoming without ever firing a shot at game in more than 20 years. It was my iron-sighted spare or back-up rifle, and had been zeroed when its Lyman receiver sight was installed about 1953. I would check the zero before each trip, but remember that no change was ever necessary. In January 1977, after a good barrel cleaning and considerable stock screw tightening, I needed two clicks left and shot a 150 + 20, in spite of heavy recoil and old eyes.

My fifteenth experimental firing was done with an Interarms Mauser rifle from Yugoslavia. I decided to test this combination with a Mauser scope from Japan, but cheated a little and had Rheinhart Fagen put a fine stock on the barreled action. The bolt and trigger are rough compared to a Remington, Winchester or Ruger, but I still fired a 150 + 24. The group was tight, but the holes in the target walked towards two o'clock after the seventh shot.

In the firing of the last two rifles, both .375 H&H Magnums, one thing stood out. A scope is an enormous aid to a hunter in the fields because it allows him to see his game and his point of impact all in the same plane. This is particularly true when a man has not been a competitive target shooter, or even if he has, and is getting old. Aperture or peep sights are seen more easily than those that are open, but not as well as with a scope. The Model 70 Winchester would have won if it had been equipped with a scope, but iron sights are more rugged.

Conclusion

We have in America today an almost endless array of satisfactory hunting rifles both new and used. The firing of even 15 delivery systems of this sort in a relatively inexact manner cannot be finally conclusive. I have purposely left out lever action .30-30's, .38-40's and .44-40's because I couldn't do them justice, but they have killed more American game than all the magnums have. The most important point may be that all 225 bullets fired from 15 widely differing rifles struck a simulated Rocky Mountain at 300 yards in fatal areas, even a relic of WW I that cost me complete less than $10.

There is, of course, far more to hunting than being able to fire prone with a sling and scope sights. The "straight shooting" quality that we all want in our arms can be secondary to weight and handiness for many types of hunting. Choose carefully according your own needs and desires.

No matter how you are armed, your results in the field will depend on your experience and practice. If you are new, learn to squeeze that trigger gently and gain confidence by firing at targets. Make sure your rifle is properly zeroed and fire carefully and slowly if you possibly can. It isn't easy to do. If you are a veteran, God bless you, but you will still miss occasionally with the best of equipment.

Shooting Muzzle Loaders

Russ Carpenter

Controversy concerning the dating of the first rifled bore will probably last forever, but it is a safe bet that, in central Europe, a lead ball was being fired from a crudely rifled barrel about the time Columbus was sailing around in the Atlantic and accidently ran into the New World. However, it was to be a couple of centuries before the rifled bore was truly understood and used efficiently.

In the early 1700's, immigrants from both central Europe and England were settling in Eastern Pennsylvania. With the Germans and Swiss the first true rifle came to the Americas. This was the jaeger or hunters rifle, and although by modern standards it was clumsy, it was accurate and, compared to other arms of the era, it was truly quite advanced. It featured a short barrel, usually about 30 inches long, and the stock was full length. The bore was seldom smaller than .60 caliber, and .75 caliber was not uncommon. The shortness and the large bore both contributed to lightness, and most jaegers weighed eight pounds, give or take a few ounces.

Among the immigrants from central Europe were gunsmiths who were soon building jaeger rifles in the colonies. However, the English had brought along graceful smooth-bore fowlers, and it was not long before these attractive lines were being incorporated in the rifles turned out by these craftsmen. The process of evolution was at work, and over the next 60 years, an all new all-American rifle came to be the standard of the frontier.

The Pennsylvania long rifle, or Kentucky as it is better known, was also effected by the economy of the times. Powder and lead were scarce and expensive, and big-bored rifles used a lot of both. For instance, there were only 15 round balls to a pound at .70 caliber, but at .40 caliber there were 70. The frontiersman was also a traveler, and to carry large amounts of lead or powder was a problem. The smaller bores were welcomed, but they were also longer. This increased the weight, but in turn, the distance across the flats was decreased, and the wood was slimmed down. This contributed to the graceful lines so admired in the Kentucky rifle.

Just before the Revolutionary War, the flintlock Kentucky had reached full evolution, and we had our first truly American rifle. How much service it saw during the revolution is argued among historians. Undoubtedly it played an important part, but the fact remains that the smoothbore musket was the standard combat weapon of those times.

The Kentucky was in its Golden Age. More than a tool of the frontier, it was a work of colonial art. Beautiful, curly maple stocks were decorated with scroll carving. Engraved inlays of silver or brass were added. In fact, many were over-decorated. However, about 1830, percussion ignition was introduced, and the decline of the Kentucky was on its way. The most beautiful of all the rifles ever made was obsolete in a mere 100 years.

True, more Kentuckies would be made, but a new rifle was developing. The Kentucky was a product of the one-man shop, but now the trend was to small factories where rifles could be manufactured by numerous craftsmen specializing in different operations. The new rifle was rather light in weight. The stock ended ahead of the forward hand hold, and the barrel was shortened to about 32 inches. While some of these rifles were decorated with silver or brass inlays, most were quite plain. The elaborate patch box of the Kentucky was replaced with a simple oval type. The earliest of these half stocks were really cut down Kentuckies, but they were easier to hunt with, and of course, less costly to build. However, the vast area west of the Mississippi beckoned, and the mountain men and trappers were exploring this territory by 1820. These men felt the need for a special gun, and the plains rifle was designed. This gun can best be described as the magnum of muzzle loaders. Tough game like bison, elk and grizzly required heavier balls, driven by greater powder charges. Of course, the needed strength made it a heavier rifle, but much of the travel in the new western territories was on horseback, so the added weight was not the problem it would have been to the earlier pioneers in the east.

This western rifle was called a mountain rifle, but today we call it the plains rifle. Whatever the name, it was truly a tool.

It was as plain as the Kentucky had been decorative. Some brass was used, but the mountain men prefered all the metal to be iron, treated to a rust-colored brown. This was insurance against a tell-tale flash of sunlight that would give away his position to hostile Indians. The barrels measured over one inch across the flats, and were usually bored from .45 to .56 caliber. Stocks were straight-grained walnut or maple. Like the better Kentuckies, double-set triggers were nearly standard. The rear trigger was the set, and it was pulled to cock when the shooter was ready to fire. The front trigger would then let off at a very light touch.

Much had been learned about barrel-making, and the long-range accuracy built into the plains rifles probably exceeded that of any earlier rifle. However, accuracy would vary with the ability and know-how of the maker, and also the shooting ability of the user.

The plains rifle was developed during the 1820's and 1830's, and this was during one of the great transitions in firearms. Earlier I mentioned the percussion cap. This was the product of an Englishman named Joshua Shaw. By 1830, most new rifles were being made with the new ignition, and many older guns were being converted. From this point on, the percussion plains rifle certainly enjoyed a hey-day, as it was recognized as the best tool in both the plains and mountains of that era. However, this great gun was to enjoy an even shorter life span than the Kentucky. The cartridge case had been perfected, and from 1875 on, hunters and frontiersmen were doing their best to trade their muzzle loaders for the new-fangled cartridge guns. Little did they realize that one hundred years later, their great, great grandsons would be trading-in their repeaters for muzzle loaders.

So far I've talked about the muzzle loader as a tool to provide food and protection on the frontier, but from the 1740's on, shooting matches were one of the few pleasures enjoyed by men on the frontier. A mark on a piece of birch-bark made with a blackened coal from the camp fire was a likely target. While rifles were loaded and targets set, a great deal of bantering took place, and in most instances, wagers were laid.

As settlements grew, target shooting became a sporting event, and much rivalry existed. By the late 1700's, match rifles were developed especially for turkey shoots. These rifles featured quite heavy octagonal barrels about 40 inches long. Double-set triggers were standard. and either peep or tube sight.

Like any sport that grows in popularity, the equipment used

always improves. By 1835, a new form of percussion target rifle firing a bullet, rather than a ball, was the gun in fashion. The bullet, called the picket ball, was a tapered conical blunt-pointed projectile with the largest diameter near the base. It was very hard to load, as its accuracy depended on the load being straight and concentric. For perfection in loading, the forward part of the heavy octagon barrel was turned round and made concentric with the bore. A bullet starter fit over this turned portion, and its plunger fit the front section of the picket ball. About 1840, Alvan Clark invented the false muzzle, and another step forward in accuracy was the result. However, loading the picket bullet was still tricky, and soon another projectile emerged. This was a long straight-sided lead bullet used with paper patching. The stage was set for some of the most accurate long-range rifle shooting the world had ever seen. Before 1840, most matches were fired at 20 rods (110 yards), but now the ranges were increased, and better groups were being fired at 40 rods than had previously been fired at the 20-rod mark. In the years that followed, matches were frequently fired at ranges as great as 200 rods (1100 yards), but 40 rods continued to be near standard. Rifle clubs were formed, and some of the greatest names in accuracy were competing—Billinghurst, Warner, Lewis, Brockway, James and others were at it until the late 1890's. The muzzle-loading target rifle had outlasted the muzzleloading hunting rifle, but for all practical purposes, muzzle loading was extinct.

From 1900 on, nearly all shooting was with cartridge guns, and for the next 30 years the only thing that kept muzzle loading alive was the tall tales of the shooting exploits of the old-timers with these guns. In the early 1930's, the tales and boasts reached a point where a group in Portsmouth, Ohio accepted the challenge, and a muzzleloading match was set to determine just how accurate the old front loaders really were. Know-how was lacking, and the accuracy was not of the bragging type, but it was the spark that set the muzzle loader on the comeback trail. From that match, which drew 67 contestants, the National Muzzle Loading Rifle Association was formed, and in the mid-1970's boasted over 20,000 members.

Other matches followed. They were held at various spots until 1942 when the Walter Cline Range was designated the permanent location on 54 acres just east of Friendship, Indiana. This range now sprawls over 431 acres, with camping facilities for 2000 registered shooters plus their families. There are ranges

for every facet of muzzleloading competition. By this I mean there are the primitive matches like those in 1740 thru 1840, but half a mile away, shooters are thumping away with the massive slug guns of the 1880's. Everything in between is here.

Through the early years of revival, interest was rather slow in growth, and then World War II interrupted, but by 1950, things were starting to roll. In the mid-1950's, I was running a gunsmith shop, and noted the increasing interest in muzzle loaders, and in turn, I started learning everything I could about these grand old guns. About that time, I attended my first muzzleloading match at Ticonderoga, New York, and I can safely say I was hooked for life.

At that shoot I met a man named Howard Blodgett, who in my opinion was one of the greatest forces in promoting the return of the modern muzzle loader in the east. Howard passed away shortly after this, but one of the things he impressed on me was the need for better rifles—the old ones were just worn out. The first thing I did after this meeting was to study the needs of the rifled bore for round balls, and I proceeded to build a rifling bench that allowed me to re-rifle old worn and rusted barrels. I did several hundred over the next few years, and by this time, barrel makers were getting on the bandwagon, and for the first time in three quarters of a century, muzzleloading barrels were being manufactured. Parts were also becoming available, and small custom shops like mine were building rifles on the pattern of those made during the past two centuries. Muzzle loading was on its way to the big time.

About 1955 a young man from Tennessee named Turner Kirkland with a lot of business sense and a love for old guns imported the first of the replicas. The gun was a Kentucky type, and was made in Belgium. Turner's Dixie Gun Works catalog for 1977 is over 500 pages thick, and lists dozens of guns, but in the 20 years after the first shipment, Dixie sold 20,000 of these rifles. And Dixie isn't the only company selling this equipment. I estimate that a couple of dozen manufacturers and importers sold 300,000 replicas in 1976 alone. This can only mean there are more muzzle loaders in use today than there were in 1840.

No doubt about it, muzzle loading is enjoying the fastest growth of all the shooting sports, so let's assume you have been

This rifle of early 1700 vintage shows the influence of the European jaeger. Note the thick grip and heavy butt stock of this replica being fired in primitive competition.

bitten by the bug and want to get started on your own. Like all things that grow fast, there are always a few fast-buck artists, and muzzle loading has its share. In many instances, it is a buyer-beware market, and any muzzleloading rifle sporting a ridiculously low price tag may well be the opposite of a bargain. In fact, some of these "bargains" may well be downright unsafe to fire. The first thing to decide is the type of gun you want to shoot, as all the rifles I mentioned earlier are available in replica form. Of course the amount and type of use your muzzle loader will get will have a great effect on your choice.

I feel the best choice for the beginner is a half-stock percussion rifle, either the lightweight New England type or the heavier plains or mountain type. You can not make your choice from the names in the catalogs, as nearly all the manufacturers and importers rely on the glories of the plains rifle for a sales pitch. For instance, nearly all the half stocks are called Hawken, plains or mountain rifles. Most of these are fine rifles, but from their names, one would think they are replicas of the type gun crafted in St. Louis back in the 1850's. These are excellent choices for most beginners, and for most hunting they are heavy enough to carry and adequate for the job. These guns are also good choices for the beginner at match shooting. True, you will soon graduate to a more sophisticated rifle, but you must start someplace. If you plan to hunt medium game like deer and black bear, I'm of the opinion that a rifle weighing about 8½ pounds and bored .50 caliber is better than a big 10- to 12-pound Hawken replica. Of course, if your ambition is to take heavier game such as elk, bison, moose or the big bears, the magnum like Hawken in .54 or larger caliber, and weighing enough to help absorb the recoil of a heavy powder charge, is the gun to pick. Undoubtedly there are hunters like the type that want a magnum for whitetails, and will pick the big plains or mountain rifle for all their hunting. For these hunters, Navy Arms offers the Hawken Hunter. Green River and Ithaca have true replicas of a Sam Hawken, and Browning is also in the market with a true mountain rifle. There are also great kits for the build-your-own-type hunter from Sharon and Green River.

If you prefer an earlier rifle, you will undoubtedly turn to a Kentucky. This rifle is required in the primitive programs and the popular rendezvous shoots, and some of the best of the conventional paper-punching off-hand matches are fired with this rifle. If competition is not your game, you will find there is no greater hunting thrill than matching wits with a foxy gray squir-

*Throughout the 1700's and early 1800's, the flintlock (left)
enjoyed its golden era. However, along about 1830, the
invention of the percussion lock (right) spelled its doom.
Ironically, the percussion lock was to enjoy a comparatively
short life, as it was replaced by the cartridge case after 1875.*

rel at first light on a frosty fall morning. Of course, the care and
feeding of a flintlock is a bit more complicated than a percussion,
but once mastered, you may never go back to the new-fangled
percussion cap.

Many replicas are available, but I have yet to see a $150 or
even a $200 Kentucky I would call a dependable rifle. Most of
these are cheap imports, and they just are not good. The best
type is a custom rifle from an experienced maker, or you can
build one from quality parts if you are handy with tools. If you
are not interested in curly wood, engraving, carvings and inlays,
you might get lucky and have an accurate dependable shooter
for about $500. Unlike the plains rifle, I know of no high-quality
Kentucky rifle kits, but plans are available, and various manufacturers offer quality parts: semi-inletted stocks from Frontier
Carving, barrels from Douglas or Sharon, locks from Siler castings, breech plugs from Luther Adkins, castings from Don Davi-

son and fittings from Ted Cash. Most of the suppliers advertise in *Muzzle Blasts*.

When you become a muzzle loader, you instantly become a hand loader. True, you don't load up a bunch of cartridges and head for the range, but on the other hand, each load you fire is built, one component at a time, in the bottom of the barrel. Like loading cartridges, different loads are made for different purposes. For instance, there is a great difference between a target load and a hunting load, but before we start loading, let's look at the necessary components.

A round ball, cast of pure or dead soft lead, is the standard projectile. I say pure lead because any impurities or other metals will increase the hardness, and while hardness is desirable when casting for a cartridge rifle, it has the opposite effect on a muzzle loader. Hard loading and poor accuracy are the results. Strange as it may seem to the novice, the round ball is the most accurate in the Kentuckies and most of the half stocks. Over the years, many bullet shapes have been tried, but because of either gas cutting or failure to stabilize in the slow twist, they failed. The great exception has been the Thompson/Center Maxi-Ball. Of course, the big slug guns fire bullets, but they are rifled to stabilize the long slugs. The Minié Ball of Civil War vintage is also a bullet-shaped projectile that fires in an accurate manner from the rifled muskets of that era.

Patching is another component necessary when loading a round ball; however, different materials can be used to gain the desired thickness. The deeper the rifling, the thicker the patch, as the grooves must be filled tightly to seal the burning gases. The material must be strong enough to allow the lands to imprint in the ball without cutting the cloth. It should be new cloth, and it should be washed to remove the starch sizing. The lightest patching is usually muslin, and at the heavy end is denim or bed ticking. It must be pure cotton, without any of the modern synthetics added. Pre-cut patches are available, but most target shooters prefer to cut their own as they load the ball. After the ball is started and is barely flush inside the muzzle, the patch is cut away with a sharp knife or straight razor. This is the most accurate method. The patches must be lubed. Although various oils (and common spit) can be used, space-age lubes and Teflon-coated fabrics are seen on the target ranges.

The only powder used is black or an approved substitute. By this I don't mean to imply a powder is good because it is colored black, and at this time there is only one substitute, which

The massive target guns of the 1880's and their replicas are thumping away in competition in much the same manner they were nearly 100 years ago. This shooter is firing one of these unlimited rifles in modern competition.

is called Pyrodex. Black powder comes in four granulations. The coarsest is Fg, and it is suitable for large-bored muskets and shotguns. Next is FFg, and the big bore rifle shooter will use this. Probably the most versatile of all is FFFg, and most rifle shooters will use this in under-.50 caliber. I even use it in my .50 caliber. The super fine is FFFFg, and the only place it is used as a propellant is in the small-bore pistols. Its main use is as a primer for flintlocks. I have also used the coarser FFFg for priming, and with a good sparking, the lock experienced no problem with ignition.

Pyrodex is called the replica black powder, and it offers several advantages, the most important of these being the lack of restrictions on storing, shipping and selling. However, it is not recommended for flintlocks, as it takes a bit more fire to ignite than the standard black. Even so, it is a welcome addition to the muzzleloading scene, as it makes a safe propellant available in some parts of the country where it has been impossible to obtain black powder.

Of course, as in conventional reloading, a primer is

needed. The simplest ignition is the caplock using the percussion cap. Caps are made in several sizes, and while not marked, some makes are better than others. Only by experimenting can you determine which is best for you. Flintlocks are a bit more complicated, but a good lock drives the flint at the right angle and with the proper force to deposit a shower of sparks in the pan as it strikes the frizzen. The amount of priming powder in the pan should be merely enough; in other words, the pan should not be full and flowing over. The touch hole should be located very close to the top of the powder level in the pan. The natural thing is to think it should be near the bottom, but this makes for slower ignition, as the priming powder must burn away before it can send fire into the main powder charge.

Earlier I likened the loading of a muzzle loader to handloading a modern cartridge. This is true, but the muzzle loader can not enjoy the variety of components employed by his modern counterpart. For instance, there is only one black powder, but the modern hand loader has several, each with a different burning characteristic. For the muzzle loader, the weight of the ball is determined by the size of the bore, and only one size will fire accurately. The modern handloader may have the choice of a dozen or more suitable projectiles.

As I mentioned, the loads for target shooting and hunting will be different. The most accurate loads are with a very tight, patched ball. Even in a clean barrel, it will start hard, but in a fouled barrel, it may be impossible to seat. This means the hunting ball must be smaller in diameter, and in turn less accurate, but it's necessary to sacrifice accuracy to insure ease of loading while afield. A ball ten to fifteen thousandths of an inch smaller will do the trick. For instance, if you're target shooting and cleaning between shots, and your rifle is a .50 caliber, you would use a .498 or .500 ball, but hunting with the same rifle, you would drop to a .485 or .490 ball.

I usually load a tight ball when I start out in the morning. Of course I use a heavier hunting charge, but my first shot will

By 1875, hunters were doing their best to trade their muzzle loaders for the new cartridge rifles. Little did they realize that 100 years later, their great, great grandsons would be trading back. This modern-day hunter traded back, and experienced the thrill of taking a pair of predators with a replica half-stock rifle.

After the bore is cleaned and charged with powder, a round lead ball is seated sprue up on a pre-lubed cotton patch. Tight fit is imperative for accuracy, but slightly smaller balls are used to insure easier loading while hunting.

be the most accurate. If things start happening and I need to re-load, I'll load the smaller ball. In the same .50 caliber I just mentioned, an accurate target load may be around 90 grains of FFg, and for whitetails it may be 125 grains of the same powder. Again a bit of accuracy is sacrificed, this time to obtain the extra killing power.

The weight of the ball is constant. Of course the undersized ball will weigh a few grains less, but as we are interested in fit, we cannot change the weight. The only time I use a scale is to check newly cast balls for uniformity. I'm never interested in the total weight, but I am interested in variations between individual balls. Any balls that weigh less than the average are remelted, as the lack of weight indicates there are internal air holes that will upset the balance in flight.

Before loading, a cleaning patch over a jag should be run down the barrel to remove oil or grease, and then a few caps should be fired to clear the oil from the nipple area. By holding the muzzle close to a blade of grass as you fire a cap, the concussion will move the grass when the channel is open. Now you are ready to load. A measure of powder is dumped down the barrel and a lubricated patch is centered over the muzzle. A ball is placed on top of the patch, and with a short starter, it is moved into the barrel. Don't be alarmed if you have to rap the starter with the heel of your hand, or even bump it with a mallet. The long end of your starter should easily move it four to five inches down the barrel, and now you're ready to seat it. Grasp the ramrod quite high, and try to move the ball all the way to the powder with one great sweep. If it doesn't work out that way, you must still make sure the ball is all the way to the powder.

Never fire a ball that is not fully seated. It is like firing a modern gun with a bore obstruction, and the results could be a catastrophe. If the ball will not move, it must be pulled, even if the gun has to be disassembled. After the ball is seated, all it takes to fire is a percussion cap for a cap lock, or some priming powder in the pan for a flintlock. Loading will take much less time to do than it takes to describe it.

Accurate shooting depends on a clean bore, and before the next round is loaded, a patch dampened with solvent should be worked back and forth with the jag end of the ramrod. A second patch will dry the bore, and you're ready to reload. It is a wise hunter who does the same, but at times this is impossible.

There is an exception to this cleaning between shots. Pyrodex produces very little fouling, and the fouling it produces does not build up, making it possible to fire many rounds without cleaning. It also allows a hunter to use a ball a mere .005 to .010 undersized.

I've saved the most unpleasant part until last, and there is no way of getting around the unpleasant chore of cleaning. The fouling from both black powder and Pyrodex is very corrosive.

After the ball is seated all the way to the powder, you are ready to seat a percussion cap. With a flintlock, it would only require a bit of priming powder in the pan. For obvious safety reasons, never seat the percussion cap until the rifle is pointed in a safe direction.

There are numerous solvents, but nothing has proven to be better than a plentiful supply of hot water. I take the gun apart, and with a patch on the cleaning jag, pump water back and forth until all the fouling is softened and pumped out. The lock and other parts can be given the same treatment, and if the water is really hot, the metal will dry almost immediately. A coat of a good lasting gun oil should protect your rifle until the next shooting session.

Muzzle loading transports us back to a far less hectic era than most of us encounter in our everyday life. To tell it all in one chapter is an impossibility, but for those who want to know more, I suggest the *Lyman Blackpowder Handbook*. It offers a wealth of technical information and know-how. Of course, there are other publications, and everyone interested in muzzle loading should belong to the National Muzzle Loading Rifle Association. A membership includes a subscription to *Muzzle Blasts,* and this alone is worth the price of membership. Write the Association at Box 67, Friendship, Indiana 47021.

Rifle Hunting

Part II

Rifles and Other Essentials

David E. Petzal

Anyone who saddles himself with a gun larger than 7mm magnum for North American hunting (unless he is going after elk specifically, or maybe even the big bears) is on the wrong track. Every year, when I make my pilgrimage west, I take two guns: a .270 that weighs 8 pounds and a .340 that weighs 10. I start out hunting filled with high resolve that I will hold out for *Cervus canadensis,* and to hell with the muleys unless they are of B&C stature.

As it always works out, the elk are in notably short supply, and I end up perfectly willing to settle for any decent mule deer. Result? The .340 sits in the cabin in the gun case, while the .270 gets to ride around on my shoulder. Please don't get the idea that I'm one of these desk-bound types who's chronically out of condition. When I pack my duffle bag, I can climb right along with the natives. But the point is, why carry a shoulder cannon when it's not necessary?

The other problem is flinch. I flinched away the one shot I was offered in the whole two weeks. There were other factors involved but, despite my long familiarity with the .340, I yanked the trigger and lost a nice deer because of it. And again, I'm not a once-a-year rifleman. I practiced with the .340 before I left, and shot some admirable groups with it. But I flinched. No one is immune. My friend Bob Brister tells me that the one time he has seen a friend of his shoot badly—a really excellent shot and a competitive big-bore shooter—was when the man had a .338 at his shoulder. No one likes to carry big guns, and no one really likes to shoot them. You may be in the best shape in the world, and you may think yourself flinchproof, but eventually it will catch up with you.

I've been picking on the medium-bores, but the .300 magnums are really no better. Just a week ago, I took delivery of a .308 Norma magnum. It weighs 9 pounds, scoped, and is stocked intelligently with a straight comb and adequate length of pull. I sighted it in along with a .338, and if there was a lot of difference between them, I couldn't discern it. It was like getting beaten on by a good heavyweight boxer, and then a good light-heavy. They both hit really hard, and you don't want to mess with either one unless it's absolutely necessary.

Indeed, as time goes on, I see less and less use for the big .30's. I own two .300 Weatherbys. (Don't ask why; I don't know either.) Both weigh about 8½ pounds custom-stocked. Both kick like mules; so much so, in fact, that they're retired, and repose in sullen splendor in the gun rack. Once you step below 9½ pounds, these guns will just about decapitate you, and if I have to carry a 9½-pound rifle around, I'd rather have one that shoots a heavy bullet.

What, you say, is the man daft? Doesn't he know that something that shoots 250-grain bullets at 2700 kicks even harder than something that expels 180-grainers at 3100? I know. But the point is that it doesn't kick that much harder, and if you're going to be shooting at something large enough to justify so much power, a 250-grain bullet is better to have than a 180. The effect of a big medium-bore slug cannot be explained in terms of figures; its effect on game has to be seen to be appreciated.

If you're skillful enough to take advantage of its extra power, the 7mm magnum can offer some real advantages. It will do anything that a big .30 will do, and with two-thirds the recoil. I have a sneaking hunch that the reason Remington sold so many is because it's the only magnum cartridge that the average rifleman can shoot really well. A hand-loaded 160-grain bullet (that weight is the best, all things considered) traveling at 3100 fps or slightly more, is a marvelously efficient projectile. And, for some reason, I've shot a lot of 7mm magnums that were real tackdrivers, but have seen few .30 magnums in the same league.

If you are set on taking an elk to the exclusion of all other game, *then* you are justified in taking a big gun. Unlike his cousins, the whitetail, muley and moose, the elk is a very tough and determined customer who can soak up a beating and run far enough that no one will find him but the coyotes. Or if you're planning on tackling a brown bear or grizzly, it pays to lug a serious rifle. But otherwise, who needs the punishment?

Should you be highly concerned about killing-power, you

can always hand load your ammunition. A .270 or a .30/06 loaded with Noslers or Speer Grand Slams is almost the equivalent of a 7mm magnum or a .30 magnum. Struck in a vital zone with one of these projectiles, the critters go down. It is far more blessed to shoot a premium-quality bullet than to burn a lot of powder. Really, if you're interested in a rifle that you can shoot, rather than merely cope with, you can't get away from the old trio of .270, .280 and .30/06.

There is another highly useful pair of cartridges that should be included in this discussion, and they are the 6mm and .243. These two seem to be controversial, and in time may generate as much heat among gun writers as the .338 and .270. I have mixed feelings, so I'll present both sides of the argument, and let you be the judge.

Those who favor the cartridges say that they are just the ticket for animals up to and including deer—flat-shooting, accurate, and with almost no perceptible recoil. In addition, both are pure hell on varmints in the off-season. You can, if you are inclined to go the custom-gun route, have a really light sporter made up for one of these loads—as light as 7 pounds, loaded, with sling and scope—and not get clobbered a bit. And, perhaps most important to our discussion, the 6mm and .243 have killed many critters with one shot.

Those opposed claim that both are for experts only; that these cartridges are only marginally adequate for a good-sized deer, and should be used only by really top shots who can place their bullets precisely. To which the "pros" reply that the light recoil allows folks who might otherwise be poor markspersons to shoot like Natty Bumpo . . . and so on, good for at least six articles per year.

My own feeling is that the 6mm and .243 have their limitations. They are fine on antelope, but not out at the really long ranges where a .270 would be far better. They will drop deer, but the big fellows, even if shot perfectly, probably will not go down as quickly as if they had been whacked a little harder. The 100-grain factory bullet, emerging from a 22-inch barrel, is only going 2900 fps or so—not exactly a powerhouse.

If you're interested in a light-kicking big-game rifle, I strongly recommend that you buy or have built a 7×57. This old-timer (vintage of 1892) utilizes the same case as the 6mm, but handles heavier bullets. No one has ever accused it of lacking killing-power (Karamojo Bell used it to kill African elephants) but you should be aware that the 175-grain factory load is for elk

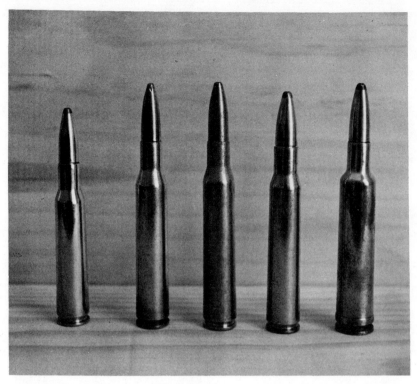

When all is said and done, these are about the best cartridges for any hunting you'll do on this continent. They are, from left: 7×57, .270, .280, .30/06 and 7mm Weatherby magnum.

and moose only. It doesn't shoot flat enough, or expand quickly enough, for general use. That long 175-grain bullet is a holdover from the original military loading. What you want is either to hand load with 140-grain bullets, or else find a dealer who carries Norma (150-grain) or Federal (139-grain) loadings. These will do the job quite nicely, and with an absolute minimum of recoil and muzzle blast.

I have become convinced of the overwhelming usefulness of the 2X–7X scope. There have been articles that state that a 4X is better for all-around use on the grounds that it is more weathertight, lighter by an ounce or two and that you don't need more than 4X anyway. I beg to differ.

First, I've never had a good scope—fixed *or* variable—leak. Years ago this might have been a factor, but not anymore. Second, who cares about an ounce or two? Nothing could induce me to clap a 3X–9X variable on a hunting rifle, or that massive

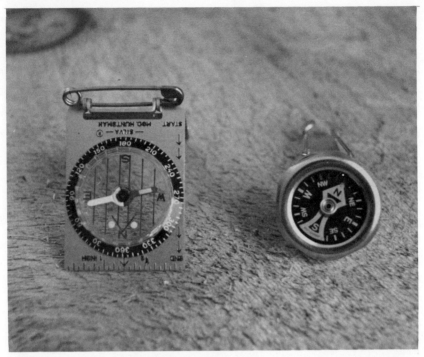

What no hunter should be without, ever. The compass at left is a Silva Huntsman; the one at right is a German copy of the Marble's pin-on model.

abomination, the 4X–12X. But the 2X7 is about the same size as a fixed 4. Most important, the ability to crank in a wider field of view or a bit more definition can sometimes make all the difference in the world.

For example, some weeks ago I was hunting in south Texas brush country, flatlands decorated with an ungodly mixture of dense brush, cactus, high grass, live oaks and other stuff too fierce to mention. If you hunt it on foot, you usually can't see more than 30 yards in any direction, and the deer are likely to be moving posthaste. In these circumstances, a 4X scope is a handicap; 2X is a godsend. On other occasions, you spot deer out in the open on the *sinderos* (pickup-truck roads) cut through the brush. There, you have the chance to shoot at ranges of 200 to 400 yards, and 7X is a lot better than 4X. Jim Carmichel, in his splendid book *The Modern Rifle,* makes the point that at long range, scopes of 6X or so are much preferred to the "standard" 4X. He's right. And the same thing applies to binoculars.

At anything over 100 yards, you'll find 10X considerably more useful than 7X.

Sometimes the little things will do you in. One of the rifles I hunted with this fall was equipped with a fine custom trigger. I have owned the gun since 1971, and it had never given me any trouble in the course of much range work and considerable hunting. One bitter cold day, the rifle refused to cock; the bolt rode home without the sear engaging. I assumed that there was not enough sear engagement, and set out to fix the trigger by adjusting the two socket-screws that regulated its movement. Guess

Among the indispensible items I carry are a drop-point hunting knife by Corbet Sigman, and one of the more elaborate Swiss Army knives by Victorinox. The latter rides in a belt sheath, although it's technically a pocket knife. In the course of a hunting trip, you may well use every blade on it.

what? My allen-wrench set was 2500 miles that way. I'd brought it out five years in a row, never needed it, and consequently left it home this trip.

Luckily, the folks with whom I was staying did have the right wrenches, so I tinkered, adding more weight of pull and more sear engagement to no avail. The problem, it turned out, was congealed matter, which could have been removed by a little alcohol. The moral is, bring a tool to fix anything that can reasonably go wrong with your gun. You may never need it, but if you do, you'll need it badly. (And it doesn't hurt to bring two rifles. My .270 bailed me out of that jam.)

Another lesson on triggers: They are adjusted indoors, where the temperature is 70-odd degrees. A trigger which is set at 2½–3 pounds feels great in a warm room, but outdoors, when it's good and cold, it's nearly impossible to control. You insert your gloved finger through the trigger guard, and off it goes, without you having anything to say in the matter. So, no matter how good it feels in the den or at the bench rest in August, resist the temptation to set the trigger super-light. A good weight is 3½ pounds, and 4 is not bad at all.

The next rules don't deal directly with shooting, but they are important. The first concerns traveling with guns via the airlines, and it goes: If there is a form of abuse that can be inflicted on a gun case in transit, it will be inflicted, and with the maximum possible force. At one airport, I once watched a baggage attendant take my aluminum gun case containing the rifles—a total weight of 28 pounds—and *throw* it through the air onto a conveyor belt. I've seen gun cases sitting out in the rain for a half-hour, propped in corners and knocked over, and so on.

In buying a gun case, you should look for a number of features. The hardware—locks and hinges—should be heavy, and securely bolted or riveted to the shell. The locks should be of the hasp-type, and should close with padlocks. The key-operated ones that I've seen are miserable. They're weak enough to be pried open by anyone with a heavy screwdriver and ten seconds; the keys are easy to lose or forget; and they're no fun to fumble with when you're having your guns inspected at the check-in counter, and thirty people are waiting in line behind you.

The shell of the case should be either aluminum or heavy polycarbonate. If the shell has any give at all to it, I'd shop around some more. There should be some sort of weather-sealing, preferably in the form of a rubber gasket around the edge of the lid. The case should not be too heavy, although you may

This is the Kalispel gun case, made of aluminum. Note the rubber gasket around the edge. The upper rifle is a .280, stocked by Jim Carmichel. The lower one is a .270, put together by Dietrich Apel.

have to sacrifice here, solid often means heavy. And it should hold the gun firmly in place. If it's a two-gun case, it will really have to clamp down hard to keep the hardware from banging together.

To date, the best case I've seen is made by Kalispel Metal Products, Box 267, Cusic, Wash. 99119. It meets all of these criteria, is not overpriced and can defy the best efforts of any baggage handler. I bought mine at Abercrombie & Fitch.

Have you been told to carry a compass? Good, I'll tell you again. This past year, I was saved great trouble and inconvenience both in Montana and Texas by having a compass along. I don't care how much of a woodsman you think you are; the minute you get deep into the boondocks, the surroundings have a way of looking the same, and then the question arises, "Where *am* I?"

A close-up of the locks on the Kalispel case. This is what should be used on all gun cases—a big, sturdy hasp that closes with a padlock.

On the first day of hunting in south Texas (mentioned earlier), the host with whom we were staying brought out a map to show us what was where. The two men who were with me—both Texans long familiar with that kind of country and with about 90 years' hunting experience between them—immediately whipped out compasses. They had them, and if you don't, you deserve whatever happens to you. The three compasses I've seen that best do the job for the nimrod are the Silva Huntsman, the Marble's pin-on compass and the pin-on made by Williams Gun Sight. All three are small, can be carried on your coat lapel and can bail you out of more trouble than you'd believe possible.

And, while on the subject of little things that can save your bacon, here are a few others. First, bring a roll of plastic electrician's tape to mask off the muzzle of your rifle when it rains or snows. The bullet will break right through the tape without being affected in any way. Until you take a header in a snowbank and fill your barrel with the white stuff, you won't fully appreciate this.

In addition to your regular hunting knife, carry a Swiss army knife. You will end up using it 15.7 times as often as the bigger piece of cutlery for everything from removing splinters to cutting moleskin for blisters.

If you hunt in cold weather, or someplace where the possibility of cold weather exists, bring along a light down jacket in addition to whatever else you have. Usually, I wear a wool cruiser, which is great—unless a high wind comes up, or unless you encounter extreme cold. As it happened this year, I found myself in the Bridger Mountains in Montana, down-jacketless, with temperature at 5° and the wind gusting up to 50 mph. What did I do? I froze. The wind went right through the wool, and if we had seen anything to shoot, I probably couldn't have hit it for shivering.

The moral is, if you're walking, stuff the jacket in a rucksack. If you're hunting out of a pickup, keep it under your seat. If you're on horseback, that's what saddlebags are for. If you're too miserable to stay outdoors, or if you're shaking too hard to aim, the best gun in the world won't help you much. Plastic tape and down jackets may not have much to do with rifles, but when it's just you and Mother Nature together, everything becomes part of everything else.

Hunting Whitetails

Jerry Kenney

A young woman friend of mine made an offer that I couldn't refuse, as the saying goes. She offered to accompany me on a hike into the Catskill Mountains of New York where I hunt, in hopes of seeing deer. What could I say? Yes, naturally.

We set out early the following Sunday morning, the day before the deer season opened in the southern zone of the state. It had snowed during the night and my camper cut the first tracks in the new snow as I turned off the main road in Forestburg into the Turner Brook Reserve and jostled and skidded up the narrow lumber trail for about two miles.

The preserve encompasses about 7000 acres, and is leased by hunting and fishing clubs, with a prescribed amount of land for each club. Besides excellent deer hunting, it offers fine trout fishing in the Neversink River, which flows within its borders.

Our parcel of about 700 acres includes Black Bear Swamp and a series of ledges and cliffs dropping steeply down to the river. Back in as far as I could drive, I pulled the truck off the trail and we got out. It was colder than we had anticipated.

We started on a trail where deer had been earlier, leaving sharp clear tracks. A short way up the trail, the meandering deer tracks moved down an embankment towards the swamp where deer can cavort with immunity. During the five years I hunted that area, we've taken deer heading into the swamp and coming away from it, but we've never been able to penetrate it. Waders and machetes would be needed, and even then it would take a week to cut through.

Where the tracks went down, we turned left along the edge of the swamp, just ambling along, talking. Twice deer ran off ahead of us. A group of three bounded into the swamp, and further on, two more tails took off uphill towards the trail we came from.

In about two hours we circled the swamp, coming out in an area overgrown with medium-size oaks. Not only was the area pock-marked with deer tracks, but the ground had been pawed everywhere by the animals scraping for acorns under the snow. It looked like they started plowing their own farm.

This came as a surprise because during the previous two years I spent a lot of time in this same spot, and it was virtually devoid of acorns then.

Twice more we pushed deer out as we strolled along looking for rubs and other signs. The deer were always well ahead of us, but we made no attempt to be quiet or sneak up on them. During the three hours or so since we started, we had seen about a dozen deer. It was very encouraging. I was already starting to change my plans about where I was going to hunt the next morning.

I generally preferred the tree-stand over on the ledges because there was almost 100 yards visibility in all directions. And I took a couple of deer from that area in the past. But I didn't get any last year, or the year before. Still, all the deer we saw that day were around the swamp, or in among the oaks scratching for acorns about a half mile from the ledges.

I was mulling this over in my mind as we started down a lumber trail that eventually would lead us back to the camper, about a mile and a half farther on. It was getting late on this November afternoon, and the sun was already down in the trees. It was getting colder, and we even jogged a little to keep warm.

We had just crossed a tiny log bridge over Turner Brook when I noticed a white flash ahead. Another tail, but it was far off and we continued walking. But I did stop when I saw two more tails much closer. Then it seemed white tails were flashing all over the place.

We moved behind a tree alongside the trail and watched, expecting to see a mass exodus of frightened does running away from us. But some were running towards us, and others were running back and forth. I realized then we hadn't spooked these deer, but something else was certainly bothering them.

One ran across in front of us not 50 feet away, and with all the commotion I wasn't really looking for antlers, but there was no doubt about this fellow. He was a good size buck with a respectable set of six-point antlers. His swollen neck thrust forward, he ran snorting with lust in his eyes. The does scrambled as he approached.

We stood transfixed at this scene while the buck raged about. For about three minutes this went on, and the buck never once noticed the strangers in his midst. But then in his blind pursuit, he ran downwind of us, and I figured any second he'd pick up our scent. Maybe he did, because he made a sharp left and came in our direction like an attacking bull. He was only about 30 feet away when he jammed his hooves into the soft snow and skidded to a stop.

The arrogant head swung up, the big donkey ears cupped and the black shiny nostrils flared. He blasted out a loud snort as if to say indignantly: "What the hell are you doing here?"

He didn't wait for an answer though. Swinging about, he tore off in the direction of the does, who had relaxed momentarily, figuring they were safe for the time being from the raging Lothario. But as soon as he started in their direction, they ran off.

After hunting in those woods for five years, I thought I knew all the runs the deer used as they ranged about the area, even though the two previous years I had been shut out—and both times I spent days in a tree-stand overlooking an area that once was productive for me. The deer used to pass through there regularly, but for some reason, they had changed their course for two years straight.

I have to admit I never thought it necessary to "survey" this area before I went out hunting. After all, I had hunted here so long, I knew the place like my own backyard. What could change? The terrain doesn't change that much—or does it? Like last year, when all of a sudden we had an abundant acorn crop.

When the rest of my hunting crew arrived, all they had time to do was sight in their rifles, a chore which I took care of a week early, for a change.

That night in camp I tried to pass on my findings about where I saw the deer for when we went out the next morning. But who wants to listen to a lecture while trying to fill out a straight or pull another jack for a full boat.

Dr. Fred Jameson from Montclair, N.J. was knocked out of the poker game early, and 10 minutes later, I was too, so I told him about the amorous buck I saw that day. Jameson had polio as a kid, and doesn't exactly spring up and down the moun-

Deer browse in different places from year to year, depending upon what's available. The canny hunter will scout the woods before the season to see where they are likely to be.

tains with his bad leg. When I told him how close to the trail I saw all this action, he made up his mind to try it.

The next morning he turned off exactly where I told him, and he found a comfortable blow-down almost within sight of the lumber trail. I went about a quarter mile further up the trail, and then down the hill about a half mile below Jameson.

The snow that fell Saturday night, enabling me to find all those fresh tracks Sunday morning, had melted in the warm afternoon sun, and by Monday morning, most of the evidence of deer was gone. I told the others exactly where I saw the deer, the signs, the tracks and the acorns. If they didn't want this advice, it was their problem. And they didn't. Not then at least.

It was a clear morning and the temperature was barely freezing. I knew by the time the sun broke over the mountain across the river, it would be a pleasant, comfortable day. From the spot I picked to stand, I could see anything that passed within 50 yards. Doc Jameson was a few hundred yards higher up, and if anything came through there, one of us should see it.

Three deer walked slowly down the hill about 7:15, but I couldn't see any semblance of antlers. Twenty minutes later, a single deer, white tail waving, bounded down, apparently frightened by one of the hunters. If he had antlers, I couldn't see them.

There was a lot of shooting that morning. Shots ranged from every direction, and a couple seemed close enough to be from our group. At 9 o'clock a loud report came from Doc Jameson's direction. I turned slowly and waited. Many times before I've gotten deer that other hunters missed, and I wanted to be ready.

There was a dark clump of rhododendron about 75 yards up the hill, and I thought I saw some movement there. There was a flicker of white, and if it wasn't a deer slinking along, it had to be a hunter wearing white socks. The deer stepped out, not appearing the least bit alarmed, and stood stone still for a few seconds. It seemed odd that if the deer was shot at, it would seem calm. It should be running into the next county by now.

I thought I saw antlers. I was almost positive, but not 100%. I don't use a scope, but I carry a small pair of binoculars, and as I put them up slowly, I saw antlers just as the buck slipped back into the brush and disappeared.

Even if I did have a chance to shoot, I would not have. Doc Jameson was right up behind that deer somewhere, and I didn't want to take any chances.

An hour later, I worked my way up to where I saw the deer, and I was surprised to find not only the deer's tracks, but a trail of blood. Ahah! Jameson did hit him. Following the blood trail, I found the doctor resting alongside a nice six pointer that he had just finished dressing out.

That explains why the deer I saw wasn't running. It was the same buck. He had been hit, and he didn't go very far before dropping over dead from a good shot through the lungs. Whether it was the same buck I saw the day before is hard to say, but it was in the same area, and it was a six pointer.

Soon after, three does lolled along, nipping at goodies, and a respectable spike buck followed at a safe distance behind. Now and then I got a glimpse of him as he moved through the profusion of blowdowns and brush, and then the three does walked out into a nice clearing and stood there, as if waiting for someone to take their picture.

Knowing the buck was on the same trail and would move out there with them any minute, I lined the rifle up where he'd come out from behind that tree, slipped off the safety and waited nervously. The does flicked their tails, wiggled their ears a couple of times and wandered off.

The buck? He disappeared into thin air. Nothing happened. I put the rifle down and stepped out slowly to see where he went, and 100 feet away from where I was looking, a white flag went up.

The Doc and I rubbed it in that night to the others, who never left their tree-stands over by the ledges, although tales of the ones that got away don't count for any points. But the next morning, the Doc went right back to the same area, armed with a special Deer Management Permit which allows the holder to take an additional deer of either sex. By noon it was tied to another buck. It was only a small spike, but a buck nevertheless.

By then we had the two opening days of the hunting season behind us and were heading home, to return two days later after Thanksgiving dinner with our families.

The Friday after Thanksgiving, John Lasher of Seaford, L.I. and I put on a short drive through the very same area Jameson bagged his two bucks. We pushed nothing out to the sitters, Tom Lacy and Dick Lewis and my son, Kevin, but only because a four pointer was so slow in getting out of his bed. Lasher almost walked up to the lazy buck before he jumped up. He took only about two leaps when Lasher nailed him.

By this time we had taken three bucks out of an area of about 10 acres, which in my opinion is phenomenal. When hunters take more than three bucks per square mile in any part of the state, the Department of Environmental Conservation wildlife biologists consider the area overpopulated with deer. If it gets any more populated in that section of the Turner Brook Reserve, we may be trampled to death.

I couldn't believe there would be any more bucks left, and the next morning I showed Kevin on the topographical map the exact location of the acorn-infested knoll where we had seen all the tracks. It was cold and nasty that day, and I decided to still-hunt around the swamp and come out near Kevin. I might push something in his direction.

It took about three hours to work my way around the swamp. I walked up on four does and pushed out five or six others, and as I rounded the far edge of the swamp, I heard a single shot not far away. I listened and saw a flash of white off to my left. Then I waited about 15 minutes before taking a step. But the first step I took was greeted by a loud snort off to my right. Another tail was up and sharp hooves were thrashing at the soft earth as I saw a head bearing two nice long white spikes clear a fallen tree and vanish in the darkness of the swamp. He must have been standing there all the time without seeing me until I moved.

I fired at the fleeing rump and after a long examination, found my slug embedded in a four-inch beech tree which it had almost cut in two. That first nearby shot still puzzled me. I gave the usual shrill whistle, and a hoarse voice answered: "Yo." It was Kevin.

From his tone I sensed he did more than shoot at a tree stump. It had been almost a half-hour since he took the shot, and when I got up to him, he was just standing over a nice spike buck. He told me he was sitting in a tree-stand when three does and two bucks came eating their way across the carpet of acorns. He picked off the last one, and the others scattered, including the spike that I shot at.

What took him so long to get to the deer, which was only about 50 feet from the tree, was his nervousness over getting his first deer.

The next day I finally did get a decent shot and once again, a spike buck. Possibly it was the spike I missed earlier. In all, we took five bucks out of an area about a half mile square. If I hadn't gone out before the season opened, there's no doubt I would have spent most of my time languishing up in that same tree-stand. Maybe I would have gotten something. Maybe not.

I'm convinced that pre-season surveys pay off. You get out alone (or with your kids), and you aren't afraid of spooking deer. You can move about more, and take time to study important signs—like rubs, tracks, droppings and feeding areas. You can cover a lot more ground than when you're hunting, because then you are always moving slowly and trying to conceal your movements.

Deer can and do change their habits from year to year, and it's usually precipitated by some change in the ecology of the region. It could be a burn-off or a severe storm that topples tall trees and brings new browse down to within reach of the feeding deer. It could also be an unseasonable freeze. Last spring temperatures dropped well below freezing for two days, killing all the young buds on the apple trees. The result was virtually an apple drought for parts of the Hudson Valley and the Catskills.

With no apples, deer had to find other sources of nourishment. In our immediate area, they found a fine substitute, a bumper crop of acorns, which are actually better than apples for deer.

They spent more time in the deep woods and oak ridges than along the fringes of the woods and in the apple orchards. They established new routes and developed new habits and hangouts. Only they don't leave any signs around pointing in the direction of their new homes. That is unless hunters can understand them.

What it adds up to is that deer change their habits from year to year, and unless the hunters change theirs, the deer are going to remain one step ahead of them.

Furthermore, taking an extra day or two to get to know your area, without the pressures of hunting, can be time well spent in other ways. Don't look on it as a chore, because you'll enjoy it. And you don't need a pretty young lady to accompany you either, although it helps.

Mule Deer Hunting

John Jobson

It is curious that even in these enlightened times, one still hears the hoary fallacy that mule deer are dumb—and if not wholly retarded mentally, at least they are much less intelligent than the Eastern whitetail. This nonsense has its roots going back to the times of Lewis & Clark when hunters used black-powder muzzle loaders, and equated killing-power with the size of the hole in the barrel.

What happened was that for generations, the whitetail had been hunted in the east by Colonists, and it was a prime protein source of the indigenous Indian tribes east of the Mississippi. The western or Plains Indians relied more heavily on the buffalo for sustenance, and the deer family (mule, elk, moose, fantail) was of more casual interest, although the buckskin was prized for clothing. At all events, the western mule deer was many decades behind the eastern whitetail in relationship with the white man and his firearms. The mule deer was innocent, the whitetail canny and knowledgeable. The whitetail, a brush and thick-woods skulker, is born with wary gamesmanship. The mule had (and still has) to learn it as he goes along.

In regard to intelligence, old John Kirk, the famous Wyoming rancher/outfitter/guide, once told me that an old mule deer buck was the most intelligent game animal in the west. Kirk was superlatively qualified to comment on such matters. I questioned him (as in those days I had always been brainwashed into believing that elk, grizzly and black bear were the smartest) and he explained. "No question," he asserted. "I have hunted them all for 50 years, and the old buck mule deer is the smartest of them all. Bighorn sheep and goats are stupid by comparison. Grizzly and black bear have their weak points if you know them.

An old bull elk is bright, too, but not like a mule deer. A mule deer can think, and he is adaptable to every situation.''

John Kirk was the type of rancher who always had his brain running well before he put his mouth in gear. His words of wisdom set me thinking along a new course, and I, from that moment, was a better mule-deer hunter, not underestimating my quarry. The mule deer gets his name from his huge ears, by the way, not from any mental association.

The mule deer has a tremendous range, being found in torrid, waterless deserts, awesome badlands, and the rolling, undulating sage flats virtually barren of trees. You find him in deep forests of the north and buffalo-grass High Plains. He's at sea level and at timberline (and above). And wherever he is found, he looks quite similar to every other mule deer in conformation. His colors (markings) may be more vivid, here and there, but you know you're looking at a mule deer when you see him. His antlers are dichotomous, or evenly branched. They fork out, whereas a whitetail has tines (prongs) emitting from one long main beam. Mule deer antlers show more singular variation than whitetail. While you know it's a mule deer, often you see them heavily palmated like fallow deer. Extremely old bucks, or ones that have had injuries to their reproductive processes, will grow a fantastic number of points and extra mass. These being classed as non-typical, nonetheless they are wonderful trophies.

Like other horned/antlered mammals, regions of limestone generally grow the hugest antlers, although not necessarily the weightiest body size. They can vary greatly. I have shot mule deer weighing over 300 pounds. Huge, grey, glossy monsters, one of which gave cut venison weighing 180 pounds. By this I mean this deer's eating meat weighed that in a Colorado locker plant. This without viscera, head, hide, hooves and most bones! There are buxom cow elk not giving any more meat. Yet I have hunted the lovely, even beautiful miniature mule deer bucks of the Belle Fourche/Cheyenne Rivers badlands in Dakota that would not field dress more than 100 pounds. A perfect mule deer in every detail, yet of sub-size. The largest mule deer I ever shot, or ever *saw,* for that matter, was at the Trumbo ranch in the Hell Creek region of Montana. He was so big, I hesitate to estimate his weight, and there was no way of weighing him. I gave most of the meat to the rancher, so have no way of knowing. But he was big! Most hunters do not even see one like him in their lifetime, and I never expect to see another coming even close to him in size. I will wager though that he was one of

Mule-deer hunting with pack horses and saddle horses in the Ruby Mts. of Nevada.

those "mythical" mule deer bucks that weight *over* 300 pounds *field dressed*.

The range of the mule deer, as we've seen, goes from the Dakotas/Nebraska to California, from Mexico to northern British Columbia, and some have been sighted in the Yukon. Some excellent mule deer are found in Alberta. The classic old notion that the best of all mule deer are those from the Kaibab country of northern Arizona and southern Utah was once valid—no more, alas, although with the adaptable, prolific mule deer, they *can* come back. Utah, by the way, once famous for mule deer, has deteriorated due, some say, to peculiar game management. I have lived in Utah for ten years, and after two attempts, I now hunt elsewhere, usually in Montana, Wyoming, Colorado, Idaho and extreme northeastern California. I have in my time hunted them over their entire general range, and all of their many environments—on foot, on horseback, 4WD and boat. I have no idea how many I've harvested, but the total is considerable. So many, a large proportion have faded from memory, and of others, only a few details remain. Yet some were such outstanding fun, I'll never forget them.

Like the time right after World War II when my family and I (wife and toddler son) drove into the hamlet of Buena Vista, Colorado in a swirling wet-flake snowstorm the eve of deer season. As we arrived, the flakes increased in intensity until they resembled the fury of a storm in a glass-ball paperweight. Gloom descended, and was punctuated by golden lights coming from windows. I knew nobody, so ducked into the local saloon and soon buddied up with an obvious local who looked like he knew the score. He was booked up, but his kid brother Will was hunting alone the next day. With facile grace, I snagged Will without further thought, and it was not a mistake.

The street light shed a candle's glow on the main drag where I was to meet Willy the next morning at 4:30. He was a minute early by my watch. He arrived in a remarkable vehicle comprised of many different truck and auto parts. The main body had been an ancient 12-to-16 cylinder (forget which) Lincoln—a mammoth affair of which he'd chopped off the roof and body behind the front seat, and made a platform there of 2-inch by 12-inch planks. The rear end, transmission and rear aheels were from some truck, looking suspiciously like a ton-and-a-half Model T. The sky was icy-cold and now twinkling. It was sharp and nippy, and I was bundled in a down jacket and scarf. We climbed steadily until hardtop turned to gravel, then dirt, then a dirt ledge road. Suddenly, Willy gave a right-turn lurch and headed up a steep, sagey mountain. We slid right back and stopped, fortunately, on the dirt track. Behind was about 2000 feet of air. We wrapped old chains around the drive wheels, wired them, and with a determined attitude, Willy gave it the lead-foot and I hung on. Somehow, the wheels took hold (the radiator was pointing nearly straight up at times) and we topped out, shooting steam, in a glade surrounded by aspen where we left the vehicle.

Dawn broke, and we followed a sharp ridge, about 150 yards

Here's the way we went at it in Elko County. We'd leave the ranch in 4×4s (either a Land Rover or a Jeep pickup, shown here) and climb to approximately the 8000 ft. level. The guide looks for deer along the way.

Use vantage points offered, and always use binoculars.

from each other. Through the quakies I saw an enormous buck surrounded by does (with other bucks hanging around, although not too close). I was shooting a Model 70 Winchester in .270 and I nailed him approximately in the diaphragm, unfortunately a bit back too far to be instantly fatal. Drunkenly, he kept his feet and headed down the mountain. The next shot got him between the hams (not the most ideal and neatest shot, but it was no time to be picky) and he rolled as he cleared a fallen log. He moved his noble head, and I mercifully shot him in the neck. This is the great beast whose mammoth head was in my Hollywood den until destroyed by fire (from a neighbor's residence). He was the most magnificent example of an all-around typical mule deer buck I've ever seen, and I've seen a few.

Other good hunts were with John Kirk in the Green Moun-

This ranch lass hunts mule deer with a Winchester 94 30/30—common on western ranches.

tains of central Wyoming. At that time, these deer ran the biggest in the U.S. in body size, closely followed by those in the nearby Medicine Bow Forest. Of course, these things come in cycles. Another memorable muley hunt was with Kirk again, out on the Red Desert after pronghorn. Kirk nudged me, and pointed to an enormous buck flattened like a cartoon cat and crawling like a cocker spaniel (and don't think they cannot) down a dry coulee. Again, the .270 rolled him, an unexpected bonus. This is the kind of deer hunting I love. While I have hunted successfully in several eastern states for whitetails (and I do not disparage them), my preference is the mule deer's open and semi-open habitat—like the juniper-dotted or piñon country of Nevada, or Utah, or the sage flats of California's Modoc country, or the same around Encampment, Wyoming. There

A happy Utah deer-hunting group. My wife, Ann, second from left.

you snug up against a small tree bole with a flat-shooting scoped rifle like a .270 with 130-grain bullet, .30-06 with 150-grain, or 7mm with 139/140-grain handy across your knees. Some lunch, canteen (for like most of the *better* mule deer country, these areas are arid) and top-quality binoculars. Depending upon how it goes, you spot the buck before he sees you, the cardinal rule of successful big-game hunting. You either stalk him, or wait for him to come closer.

A hunt I'll never forget was the aforementioned one for the small, perfectly proportioned bucks of western South Dakota in the Belle Fourche-Cheyenne watersheds. These little rascals were sleek as knockwurst and grey as wolves. It is unspoiled terrain with great, flat, winding river-meadows surrounded by a maze of torturous canyons and "breaks" with sharp ridges—

Opposite
Small muleys are not to be sneered at.

Horseback country. Jobson in front.

from whence, once, Indians hunted; next, cowpokes rode ponies checking on the herds from a fine vantage point; and now they do the same with 4WD. That's the way they hunt these mule deer. My guide, Glen Speer, took me far along one ridge, and I de-rigged. He drove away telling me to wait until the furor of the grinding gears abated, and then walk back several miles eye-balling the coulees from atop this winding ridge. I did so, and shot a simply wonderful, although diminutive, mature, typical buck. My wife did the same. These deer were only slightly bigger than the little Coues whitetail of Sonora. For deer, you just can't beat those .270's, as has been said in truth since 1926.

Since mule deer are so adaptable, it is hard to say exactly what *all* mule deer habitat is. It likes lands more arid, open, and rougher than the whitetail. Even in the west, the whitetail hangs around the brush and trees of flat river bottoms. Not the mule! He goes as high as sheep, and he likes to see far. One area in which the *average* mule buck differs from the canny whitetail is that he sometimes will stop for one last look, like many western and African animals. This has been costly to many of them. Most whitetails keep going. The mule, like most game animals, has one weak point, and in the case of very old, big-antlered bucks, this has led to their downfall by unscrupulous "sportsmen" (including a surprising number, I understand, of my peers and colleagues, some of whom, apparently will go to any lengths for a story). While this doesn't get into the outdoor magazines so much (obviously), it is a fact that mossy-horn old deer can be had by the infamous practice of jacklighting. I have seen many monster buck supposedly shot right after legal opening, and anyone can tell this type has been long dead. They are stiff, and the eyes sunken. There are other signs. They were killed illegally by spotlight the previous night, or night before. I have lucked into several outstanding racks, but it was always in fair chase. Most of my mule deer have been typical bucks from two-to-three years old on to eight years of age.

It is common these days to combine a mule deer hunt with another species, like pronghorn or elk. Pronghorn habitat is often excellent for mule deer, but elk compete with them. Yet, they are there.

Most of us like the wide-spread antlers, yet some prefer those that grow more vertically. Both are good, and probably the

My pal, Tom Billiard, scoping for muleys.

vertical-pronounced type are the better fighters, but there is no question that the wide massive antlers are most colorful and noble. Some have gone to well over 40 inches in spread, and when you figure a worthy Wyoming moose is 50 inches, you get the idea. Any mule deer buck with a spread well over 30 inches was not behind the door when they passed out the brains.

These deer lie where it is virtually impossible to approach them without them seeing and scenting you. They bed in shelter (tree or rock) where they can see all sides but up. You can't get to them from below. Your only chance is to go *above* (for these old-timers) and pussyfoot along, pausing frequently, for lengthy pauses. Do not try to cover a lot of ground. You'll never walk up to a smart mule, unless he's so old he's deaf. Not likely, or a mountain lion (their natural enemy) would have long ago had him. It helps to toss stones at likely looking clumps of brush, or overhanging rimrock. Sometimes a big old buck will bolt like a cottontail, and it pays to have your rifle at the ready. I have seen countless old bucks in the edge of aspen groves, or scattered fir, on a point. The air, warmed by the sun, rises and gives them a dandy smell of any trouble coming from below. They can hear like kudus. Spooked, they will start in one direction until out of sight, and then swap ends on you. I have seen them many times (through binoculars from afar) work around *behind* a hunter where they can keep their eye on him. It is most amusing. One fellow I saw went around a clump of greasewood, and the buck kept on the opposite side. It was snowing, so the hunter saw the buck's tracks as well as his own.

The frustrated hunter changed directions. So did the deer. At last the hunter threw down his rifle, flung his cap on the ground and stomped on it. That deer, gambling with his life, was toying with the hunter. He got away. This took place in sight of a town of 8000.

Most elderly bucks are loners. They shy from does and fawns unless it's the rut. Sometimes one will team up, like elephant and Cape buffalo, with a younger buck. In return for educating the younger one, he gains the benefit of youthful eyes, ears and nose. In bad weather, though, a bunch of old bucks may foregather. Once in the High Uintas I saw nine or ten old bucks all together, sociably, and it was fair weather. So there are no hard and fast rules.

Although there are some whitetail deer (like, say, in Minnesota and maybe Maine, Michigan, and parts of Pennsylvania and New York) bigger than some mule deer—as a class,

The horns of an enormous mule deer buck killed by my friend,
Lynn Lutz, near the Wyoming/Utah border.

as a species it has been my experience that most mule deer run bigger than most whitetails.

And there is no question that most mule deer are bagged at far longer ranges than whitetails. In fact, a lot of mule deer are shot across canyons and far out on the sage. You need the flat-shooting rifles I mentioned, or the equivalent. You do not require a magnum, though if you have a Weatherby .257, it does not hurt. I have shot deer with that, the 270, .30-06, 7mm, .25-06, .257 Roberts, and I've seen many shot with those plus 250/3000, 6mm, .243. A good rifle scope is a must for efficient western shooting. Young eyes can do with a top 3X (3 power). A four power is ideal. Some need six if they are long-acquainted with use of rifle scopes.

No doubt, since about 1900 until now, more mule have been killed with a 30/30 saddle rifle/carbine than any other caliber, and not a few have been taken with the old .35 Remington, the great eastern deer cartridge that deserves all the praise you can give it for a brush gun (i.e. short range). But again, the 30/30 has likewise wounded and lost about as many deer as it has taken—not so much because of its muzzle energy as because it is not an accurate long-range rifle/cartridge combination. Yet, the 7/57 (7mm) Mauser with 139-grain bullet is one of the top all-time-best mule deer cartridges ever made, and it is not that much more hefty than a 30/30. It is usually shot in a scope-sighted rifle by one who knows the rudiments of marksmanship. Undoubtedly the one best mule deer caliber is the .270 with 130-grain (not 150-grain) bullet closely followed by the .30-06 with 150-grain. Somehow, I do not get excited over either the .308 or the .300 Savage, but then that's what makes horse races. Sight in a .270 for 250 to 275 yards. Then no matter how far the deer seems in the clear air, hold dead center on the chest, at least for the first shot. You'll hit a lot more often than you'll miss!

Rattling Up Deer (and Other Secrets)

Bob Brister

The battered red "rattling horns" clashed together one more time, trying their best to sound like a couple of bucks fighting over a doe, but starting to lack conviction. They had been through the same routine of hit, twist and pull apart for hours in the cactus-mesquite country near the Mexican border in South Texas.

But the only thing moving was a big red-tailed hawk, circling and hovering over a once-cleared grassy field to my left. I watched him with binoculars, wishing I had his elevated view of the dense thicket beyond him. He was hovering low, probably trying to nail a blue quail, when a movement behind in the brush attracted my attention to a tiny opening in the mesquite. Probably a bird; the South Texas brush is full of them.

But there he was, head and shoulders out of the brush, antlers shining in the sun. My pulse always pounds at a time like that, and if it ever stops, I will quit hunting. The thrill of "rattling up" a buck—any buck—is enough. But the possibility of a record-class trophy adds a lot to the sensation, and I knew I was in "monster country."

I braced the binoculars on my knees, wishing they were my 10×50 Bushnells instead of the lighter but less powerful 7×35's. As the glasses settled down and sharpened into focus, reason returned. He was a good buck, a fine, heavy-horned 10-pointer judging from the side of the rack I could see. But he was certainly nothing for the record book, and for that matter, I hadn't really rattled him up anyway. He was nearly a quarter mile over there, and as I watched, he dropped his head to feed at the edge of the field. Even if he had been able to hear my rattling efforts,

This buck came from behind, recognized his mistake at the last minute, and jumped over the clump of bushes in which Brister was hiding. In another split second, he was gone. To get off a shot in such circumstances, horn rattler must have rifle, not antlers, in hand.

he wouldn't have stopped to feed if he was really on his way to a "buck fight."

Or would he? I eased the antlers into position, made sure they were properly lined up to mesh solidly without pinching a finger, and hit them together hard as I could, twisting and pulling to get as much sound as possible.

Instantly the buck's head came up, and he seemed to look straight at me. Then he took a couple of hesitant steps forward. He could hear those horns! I clashed them again, and he took a few more steps, now clear of the brush but confronted by the wide-open field. No big buck, I figured, would cross that open expanse in the middle of a bright afternoon.

He just stood there, looking and listening. I looked at my watch. Although it seemed I'd been sitting dead still for an hour, the watch showed I'd been there 25 minutes.

It was a wonderful lesson in the most common mistake

In very early morning or late afternoon, bucks are more likely to cross openings, and can normally be "rattled" from a greater distance. Still days are better than windy ones because the sound of antlers can be heard farther, and human scent is not carried so far downwind.

made by almost all of us who attempt to fool bucks into coming to what they believe is a battle over a sex-ready doe. I would have almost certainly moved on to some other location had I not happened to see him when I did. And even from that distance, he would have almost certainly seen me and melted into the brush the moment I moved. Thus, I would have moved on, unaware I'd rattled up a deer. How many times have I done that?

Lots of times, probably. Two of the best deer rattlers I've hunted with, veteran guide Bob Snow and Charlie Schriener (owner of the famed YO Ranch near Kerrville, Texas) agreed that for every buck rattled up, probably two or three others sneak up and see the hunter first. With an inexperienced hunter, the odds on that increase because beginners often pick a poor spot to do the rattling (where a deer can see them without leaving the brush).

No buck in my 20 years of experience at rattling deer ever

*This is a typical Texas buck coming to horns ready to fight.
Note swelled neck accentuated by "hackled up" hair. The
young eight-pointer is probably less than three years old.
Older, wiser bucks are less likely to come clear of cover.*

gave me a better lesson on the value of patience, or perhaps in
how far a buck can hear rattling horns, than that buck on the
Brock ranch in Starr County, Texas.

It is rare to be able to observe a buck's reaction to horn rattling at a great distance, because bucks usually are in enough
cover that you can't see them from very far away. This one
seemed to have very mixed emotions. He would stop, look, listen motionless for several minutes, then start grazing again. But
when I hit the horns, he would throw up his head and move a
few steps forward. Once he was out into the open field, his mind

This buck is sneaking downwind in a circle, keeping head down and holding to cover, a typical maneuver of an old buck who trusts his nose more than ears or eyes. The photo was made by Brister hiding some 30 yards downwind of a companion who was doing the horn rattling.

seemed to be made up, and he began to trot toward the protection of the brush on my side.

He had slightly misjudged the location of the sound, and was angling too far in front of me, or perhaps he wanted to get well downwind of the "action" to check it out. In either case, his direction would put him just downwind of me, and I figured the first scent of man would send him barreling into the brush on my right. So the decision had to be made in a hurry. And the closer he got, the bigger the rack looked. He was starting to lope, anxious to get across that opening.

The cross hairs found him, moved out ahead of his shoulder, and I started to squeeze. But moving shots are easy to miss, and there's often no need for them. I whistled as loud as I could, trying to make him stop. It was a pretty poor whistle, and I don't think he heard it. Then I yelled "hey," and he skidded to a stop and looked straight at me. The 165-grain Speer Grand Slam hand load broke his neck, and if he kicked, I never saw it.

It was, in other words, the sort of clean, one-shot kill we all try to make. But more than that, it was a good lesson for me in the relative effectiveness of horn rattling.

That particular ranch is not at all crowded with deer. One friend of mine has hunted dove and quail there for years, and has never even seen a doe, much less a buck.

For days prior to my hunt, several other guests had hunted from elevated blinds. They had seen a few deer, but had killed only one buck. For me to simply walk out on foot the first afternoon and kill a big, heavy-beamed buck within three hours was

Hidden in shade of brush clump, using dead log to hide movement or horns, one hunter takes aim while the other rattles. Horn rattler purposely raised horns for photograph; otherwise they would be kept low to the ground to reduce the chance that the buck would see movement.

Meshing tines "front-to-front" is method favored by many horn rattlers, but can pinch a finger, particularly when ends of the tines are not removed. A mistake here would mean a pinched right forefinger. Note camouflage mesh jacket, a great aid in breaking up hunter's outline.

not consistent with the "odds." Other guests had spent more than 50 man-hours of silent, observant watching of the brush. The indication was that horn rattling, which can make a buck move when he otherwise wouldn't be moving, is sometimes more "efficient" than sitting in a stand—at least when conditions are right for rattling.

The next morning tended to confirm that theory. Ranch owner Bill Brock and I hunted together, and I rattled up and killed a big 8-pointer before 8:00 A.M. Those were the only two bucks I saw the whole trip. Nobody else even saw a buck that last day. Perhaps, had I not been rattling horns, I would never have seen one the whole trip.

But before you rush out and begin bashing antlers together, let's put this method of game-calling into perspective. Had I rattled horns some other weekend of the season, other than the last one, when South Texas deer are normally at the peak of rutting activity, I might never have seen a buck. Had I rattled horns on some ranch with a population of twenty doe per buck, I would not have rattled up many (if any) bucks. This ranch, although with a relatively low deer population, apparently has an excellent buck-doe ratio. Ranch workers say they see almost as many bucks as does. And this is a very vital statistic to horn rattling.

Nature intended deer herds to be just about 50-50, bucks and does, and that is the sex ratio of fawns at birth. Since one buck can breed a lot of doe, nature uses the resulting competition to insure that the buck doing most of the siring in his territory is the strongest and smartest buck around. This is nature's way of upgrading the genetic qualities of the herd.

Obviously if overhunting of bucks, and underharvesting of doe, has put the sex ratio so out of balance there is little competition among bucks, there will be little fighting, and little chance that rattling horns will call up a deer. That's why it is difficult to rattle bucks in many areas of the country where doe hunting is prohibited.

In purposely posed picture, several "no-no's" of horn rattling are portrayed. Shiny gun against tree is like a warning beacon to a buck, and shiny objects such as rings or watches can have the same effect. Note cord that connects bases of rattling antlers; this is convenient for carrying them slung over a shoulder between rattling locations. Antler tines were sawed off and blunted to make them safer to carry and easier to use.

This young buck appears to be walking on eggs, literally tiptoeing up to the sounds of a mock battle. He probably has aspirations of stealing the favors of the doe in question, but doesn't want to risk an encounter with larger buck. This buck repeatedly pounded the ground with his forefeet, then watched apprehensively to see if anything came charging out. If larger buck appeared, he would have departed instantly.

I've written a number of articles about rattling for deer over the past 20-odd years, and I've always tried to make clear that it is not magic, not something for a few sophisticated, gifted "experts." In pure technique of making sounds, it is not nearly as difficult as duck calling, and anyone with enough coordination to hit two deer antlers together can, under the right circumstances, rattle up a buck. Yet the best guide going can't rattle up a buck when the buck doesn't want to come to the "fight."

Even in areas with a lot of deer and competition among bucks, there will be days when rattling horns seems as utterly

This buck's freshly cut ear was probably received in a battle with a bigger buck the same day, but he was brave enough to come to the rattling horns, and even after seeing he had been tricked, stopped for one last hopeful look backwards for a doe.

foolish as it looks. The deer just won't come. And then, maybe the next morning, several bucks will come, occasionally two at a time.

I cannot explain that, but it could be that the "doubles" occur because each buck knew the other was in the adjoining territory. I believe it is much easier to rattle up a buck when he knows he has competition right over the hill.

Why do bucks want to fight one day and not the next? Nobody knows, but it undoubtedly has something to do with another batch of doe coming into heat. Contrary to popular belief, the so-called "rut" does not occur all at once, nor for all doe. I've worked with biologists checking fetal development of doe taken during hunting season, and some of the older doe were found to have been bred a month or more earlier than others. There is apparently a "peak period" of rutting, when mature doe come into estrus, but (fortunately for the breeding bucks) even then the females don't become receptive all at the same time. Young doe, late maturing yearlings who were born late the previous spring, may come into heat a month or more after the early rut.

Your state game biologist can tell you the general period of rutting activity in your state. Some states apparently purposely set deer season to miss the rut, and if you live in one of those states, you won't be rattling up many bucks.

If you can hunt during rutting season, remember that a period of cold weather seems to accelerate activity, and a good time to go is just before, or after, a cold front hits. It is true, as biologists can prove, that doe come into estrus primarily in relation to the length of the days (their "body calendar" depends upon hours of daylight). Yet cold weather appears to bring on the daytime breeding activity observed by hunters and game management workers. What the deer do at night is their business.

In all of this I am saying "deer" and meaning whitetails. Mule deer are different in that they are not territorial animals, or do not stake out a territory with "rubs" and "scrapes" as whitetails do. A "rub" is where a buck polishes his antlers. A "scrape" is where a buck has pawed the ground and urinated upon the dirt to leave his message, just as a dog marks a bush by raising his leg. Whitetails tend to do both of these things within their "territory," whereas mule deer will clean their horns wherever a limb happens to be handy. They do not defend their territory against other bucks, and thus are said to be impossible to rattle up with antlers.

I do not believe rattling mule deer is impossible, because I have done it (before witnesses, by the way). But I've decided long ago it is generally "impractical" to rattle up a mule buck because you have to be lucky enough to catch one when he is actively rutting, but has not yet located a doe to follow. A whitetail, under similar circumstances, is so territorial and belligerent by nature that he may (like a bull elk) challenge an intruder in his territory, regardless of whether or not he is at that moment actively looking for another female.

I asked one of the outstanding deer biologists in America, Dr. Al Brothers of the Zachary Ranch near Laredo, Texas, what he thought of statements that mule deer cannot be rattled.

"I think any antlered animal that fights over females can be attracted to a simulated fight," he said. "The whitetail is just easier than most because he is so territorial."

Apparently I've been unusually lucky (or tried an unusual number of times) because I've rattled up muleys in several states, two in one morning on the Jicarilla Apache Reservation in New Mexico. But on that same trip, afterwards, I rattled my heart out for four days and never got another buck to come up. My surmise, after that experience and several others like it, is that I won't waste much time rattling for mule deer, unless I'm lucky enough to be in good country where there are a lot of bucks, at the right time of year, and when the weather puts them actively into a rutting mood. Mule deer doe, incidentally, seem to be more curious about horn rattling than whitetail doe. Many times I've had them pop up over ridges and watch me. But admittedly those deer might have done the same thing had I been sitting on a stump playing a harmonica. Muleys are notoriously curious, and I've read that both bucks and doe can be called with predator callers. I've never tried.

The most important element in selecting a rattling site for whitetails is a fresh "sign" indicating a buck is using the area. Rubs (where antlers were cleaned) are the most common sign seen by hunters because they are the easiest sign to see. But "scrapes," those little pawed out places in the pine needles or dirt, mean a lot more. A doe in heat supposedly seeks out such scrapes, and will urinate on the same spot, thus leaving her signal that she is in the area and in a friendly frame of mind. A buck is said to travel his markers much as a trapper runs his lines, and if he finds fresh sign of a doe, he will trail her (head down and to great extent oblivious of everything else) until he either sires her next year's fawn or gets into a fight trying.

Whitetails fight a lot, as is evident if you closely examine bucks killed during the rutting period. Lots of them will have cuts and bruises which are not like those a deer gets from going over or under fences. On one ranch I once hunted, the manager had a collection of "locked" deer horns he'd found after both animals, or one, died as a result of a fight. Another friend of mine has a beautiful mount of two whitetails fighting; that's the way he came upon them, and he killed both. They were both about finished, the larger one dragging the almost lifeless loser locked to him. My friend probably did them both a favor, because it is doubtful anyone could have freed them.

When antlers are locked like that, it is all but impossible to separate them without breaking a tine. The power that was required to lock those antlers so securely is significant in that it indicates how hard the animals hit together in battle. I've read horn rattling stories in which the writer suggested making very low sounds with the antlers, just "ticking" them together for calling in close deer (just as some advocate blowing a duck call with less volume when birds are close). But a duck is a duck, and a deer is a deer, and I believe in sounding as much like either one, whether the distance is near or far. I've never had any trouble spooking close deer by hitting rattling horns together hard, but I have had several "close deer" come so quickly that they caught me with the horns in my hands. One of those jumped over the brushpile I was in, another jumped into a pile of logs with me and right back out again before I could do much more than blink. Another I saw coming in time to grab the camera (I was rattling for pictures that trip) and I made a picture of him sailing over.

Frankly I don't think it makes a great deal of difference whether horns are rattled loudly or softly, except that hitting hard sends out the sound a little farther. Neither is there any special cadence to rattling, just so long as it vaguely resembles the three basic elements of a deer fight, the loud clash as they first hit, the clashing, gnashing sound as they twist their heads trying to throw the opponent off balance, and the pulling apart sound as they back off and square off again.

One evening a few years ago Walter Fondren of Houston and I got into one of those late-evening deer-camp discussions over horn rattling, and never could agree on precisely how the horns should sound. He said I made too much noise, and I said he didn't make enough. Next morning we both went out and rattled up bucks, although I must admit the heavy-beamed 13-pointer he called up for his wife Fran was bigger than anything I saw that day. My only claim to fame was rattling up two nice 8-pointers at once for his son Leland, the second time in two I'd rattled up "a double" for that youngster. Thus I suppose Leland Fondren figures I know something about rattling up deer, and Fran Fondren figures her husband knows best. Much of the lore of horn rattling revolves around success, and if one hunter is lucky, or hunts a good area, or knows his deer sign language better than another hunter, his rattling technique is the one that is likely to be copied by others. Along the Mexican border, I've watched natives rattle, and it consists of nothing but putting the horns together, hitting a couple of licks, and that's it.

*The instant an old buck realizes he's been "had," he will bolt
for heavy cover; unless hunter is ready, he'll never get a shot.*

Up in the Hill Country around Kerrville, I've seen guides
effectively demonstrate elaborate displays of rattling, including
scraping bark off trees, rolling rocks, thumping the ground with
the back of the horns, breaking brush and creating a real production of a deer battle. Obviously when two big bucks fight, a
lot more things happen than just antlers clashing; they really tear
up the territory.

I've tried all of this and found that, for me, the things that
work best are a moderately short rattling session, a few thumps
against the ground to simulate the hooves of deer, and if it's

handy, I'll roll a rock, or whip a bush with the horns to make some more noise.

But the important things are to be still instantly afterwards, and to make sure the deer doesn't smell you. To do that, you either plan the rattling location well, or mask your scent.

Some old-timers swear by skunk scent, a commercially available potion (from Burnham Bros, Inc. of Marble Falls, Texas) that smells like hell. The common way to use it is to open a bottle downwind of your rattling position. The smell of a skunk isn't frightening to a deer, and it helps mask your smell.

Whatever the rationale, "skunk juice" works, not just with rattling deer, but with calling up a lot of animals, including coyotes, closer than what might be described as "normal smelling distance" of *Homo sapiens.*

The only trouble with skunk juice is, if you make a mistake and get some of it on you, it's pretty durable. I've found the safest way to avoid this is to dip a couple of cotton "Q-tips" into the skunk scent. Then just break off the sticks so that the cotton tips fit into a separate bottle that can be tightly capped. That way you don't have to carry around a whole bottle of liquid that could spill when you open it. The soaked "Q-tips" will hold plenty of non-spillable stench.

Some hunters cut off the musk glands of killed bucks, and put these in a jar for this same use. This must indeed be a convincing smell to a buck sneaking up on a phoney battle, particularly if the musk glands (those little black, stinky tufts of hair on the inside of a buck's hind legs) were removed from a buck in full rutting aroma. Bucks urinate on these tufts to add scent to their message to doe.

Should you decide to try to use the musk-gland gimmick, just remember that the jar must be kept quite cool or the glands will spoil—and if they do, I don't think the horniest buck in America would come to antlers rattled behind such a stench.

Deer tend to trust their noses more than their eyes, and thus it is important to select a rattling site with an opening *downwind* of the hunter. A smart buck will usually circle to try to get a whiff of what is happening, but he doesn't like to cross openings, so the odds are good he won't cross your opening and pick up your scent. However, if thick brush is directly downwind, he can maintain his cover and usually will smell you before you can see him. If he does step out into the opening downwind, try not to move while he's looking for you. Wait until he turns his head or starts to move; he won't catch the movement of raising your gun quite as easily when he is also moving.

Camouflage-clothing, at least shirt or jacket, is a definite advantage, because it helps break up your outline. A big cowboy hat is not exactly camouflage, but I wear one when I'm hunting in Texas (and some other western states) because I'm accustomed to that kind of hat, and because the game is, too. Deer see ranch workers every day, year around, in cowboy hats, and perhaps pay a little less attention to them than they would someone wearing an African pith helmet. I can't say deer are that smart; I can say they definitely become accustomed to human activities that they do not associate with danger.

When I'm rattling horns, and don't feel I'm well enough hidden by brush, I take off the hat and put it on the ground beside me. I wear it while walking, because when I'm walking, a smart buck is going to see the movement (and me) anyway.

I try to walk quietly and slowly and hold to cover while moving from one rattling location to the next, very much the same as if I were "still-hunting." But if I know I can't cross an area without being seen, I try to walk fairly quickly and casually, as if I were going about my business on the ranch. I resume stalking in the next heavy cover. I've killed a lot of deer on horn-rattling hunts when I wasn't actually rattling horns, just easing up on them as I would if stalking or still-hunting. That is one value of the rattling system; it permits covering a great deal of territory, affords the chance to use binoculars on the cover ahead, but it still offers the option of making a buck move out of heavy cover toward the horns—when that buck probably would never be seen otherwise.

Some hunters wear camouflage-clothing but carry around a gun that shines like a mirror. I believe they might as well wear a silver space suit to match the rifle. Nothing spooks deer more than a flashing surface. My favorite "rattling rifle" is a short, light .308 with oil-finished stock and non-reflective bluing. If I'm really serious in trophy-buck country, I wrap it with camouflage bow-tape, the kind normally available in archery shops.

In photographing hunters, I've noticed the shine of a rifle is the first thing the camera's eye (or mine) picks up at a distance. A white human face is also a dead giveaway in a dark thicket, and for the really serious hunter, Penn Woods Products, Inc. now offers handy camouflage face paint that comes in tubes, and washes off easily with soap and water. Just remember that the

A buck often just "materializes" without a sound, and if horn rattler makes a move while he's watching, the deer disappears, and hunter never knows he has rattled up game.

same gimmicks of camouflage that are important to turkey hunters are important to deer rattlers. Any time you are calling a smart animal *to* you, he is going to be looking *for* you, and there is more need for camouflage than if you were just walking through the woods jumping game.

Some rattlers prefer to hunt in pairs, one doing the rattling and the other sitting back-to-back, so that all directions can be covered without twisting around to look (as a single hunter has to do to see behind him). Any movement is bad, and almost any way to minimize it is worthwhile.

Nevertheless, I personally prefer to hunt alone most of the time. Hiding one person at a rattling location is easier than hiding two, and there is less likelihood somebody will move when the buck happens to be looking. It is also quieter moving from one location to the next, and one human presumably smells half as bad to a buck as two humans.

In areas where very heavy cover is cut through by fence-lines, pipeline crossings and old roads, the intersections of such openings are excellent locations to rattle, and these are good to work with someone else. One hunter can be stationed to watch one opening, say a fence-line running north-south, while the other hunter can watch the opening running east-west. This doubles the odds that one or the other will see a buck sneaking across an opening, and in such places, that is usually the only chance you'll have—although I have seen bucks come charging up the middle of a ranch road looking for a fight.

There is no way to say how a buck will come to the horns, sometimes he'll be on the run, all hackled up and wild-eyed; sometimes he'll be sneaking along so slowly he just materializes.

It is fun to watch the young bucks and "spikes" who obviously would certainly like to meet a nice doe (or steal the one the big boys are fighting over) but have no desire to encounter Mr. Macho. A spike buck that has no real fighting equipment often will appear as if he is walking on eggs, really slipping along. Then he may stop, loudly stamp one foot against the ground as if in challenge—then quickly look around him like a scared kid who just yelled "chicken" at the town bully. If a big buck shows up, the little one will take off.

In general, the most likely bucks to come to horns will be those with good body size and antler development, but not much age. Rarely will a really old buck come rushing in rashly to see the fight. He is the one who will circle downwind and just materialize. The next move you make, he'll give you a glimpse of massive antlers as he takes off through the brush. Rarely will you get a good shot unless you're good enough (or lucky enough) to see him before he sees you.

Never base any general conclusions of horn rattling on the reactions of any one buck. You may see a distant buck feeding, rattle the horns and he'll raise his head a moment and go on feeding. He isn't interested. Sometimes he may even spook and run off into heavier cover. Or he may turn and come for you on the run. But whatever the reaction, it has little bearing on what that same buck may do the next day, or the next week, or maybe when he's been trailing a doe into some other buck's territory.

I've heard the comment that horn rattling may be OK in Texas, but won't work elsewhere. But I, and many others, know better. Biologist Al Brothers, who wrote a terrific book about deer entitled *Producing Trophy Whitetails*, mentions that he has received reports from all over America of unsuccessful horn rattling. He believes it can be done anywhere there are whitetails. But certainly some areas are a lot easier than others, and Texas is one of the best (at least some areas of the state) because it has so many deer.

If you hunt where there are very few deer, the odds are lower of rattling up a buck because the deer are less accustomed to buck fights—and for that matter, odds are poorer of seeing a buck no matter how you hunt.

If you hunt very, very thick cover, such as some of the swamplands of the Deep South, rattling is less likely to succeed because the deer can get close enough to smell you before you can see him. You might try rattling from a tree-stand, because human scent is less of a problem if the source is high above the ground. Also you can see a buck coming at a greater distance.

Sitting in the same elevated stand all day and rattling isn't very efficient because you aren't covering much territory. Although I'd rather have my rattling horns in a tree than to be sitting there depending entirely on random luck to bring a buck by.

I've rattled up bucks at all hours of the day, but early morning on a calm, crisp dawn just after a cold front is "prime time." Another good time, believe it or not, is in the middle of the day when deer are normally bedded down in heavy cover. If you know where such heavy cover is, sometimes you can make a buck come out during a time of day when other forms of hunting might be wasted time.

If you don't believe very strongly in horn rattling, try your usual form of hunting during the early morning and late after-

This South Texas buck was rattled up and killed at less than 25 yards. Author's cowboy hat is often removed during rattling sessions, but is worn walking between locations. He believes deer accustomed to such clothing worn by ranch workers are less spooked by it. In crossing openings, walking to next rattling spot, he stands erect and walks fast and casually. To bend over and obviously sneak along is more likely to spook deer which might otherwise stay put in cover and let ranch worker go by. Spooked doe or other game encountered en route to next rattling location will almost invariably alert game ahead. If hunter sees doe or small bucks along the way, he should keep walking and act as if they weren't there.

noon periods when deer are moving most—and try rattling around heavy cover in the off-hours. You may be surprised, and at least you haven't wasted valuable time on a gimmick you're not convinced will work.

I've never tried to "sell" horn rattling to anyone; if you want to try it, fine. But if you do, give it a fair chance. Remember that you didn't kill a buck the first time you sat on a stand or walked through the woods, either. The more rattling you do, in most locations, the better the odds are that you'll call up a buck.

If you don't have an old set of buck antlers, you may be able to acquire some from your local taxidermist, or rob some moth-eaten old mounted head in the attic. I don't subscribe to the idea that rattling horns must be "fresh" to be natural sounding. They can be soaked in water, or rubbed with linseed oil repeatedly until some of the "tinny" sound goes away. But most of that tinny sound comes from holding the antlers wrong. I've rattled bucks with whitened "pick up" antlers discarded by some buck the year before.

Remember that antlers are very solidly attached to the head of a live buck, so hold the bases tight enough to dampen the vibrations. Holding them too lightly can make them click like dry sticks. I usually wrap the base of my rattling horns with tape, creating a comfortable "ball" for a hand grip at the base of each antler. This dampens "tinny" vibrations, and also cuts down on some of the shock to your hands when you clash them together.

No pair of antlers meshes together exactly the same way, and you have to fool around a bit to see how yours go together best. You may find that one works best in the left hand, or vice versa, and if so, mark them so that you know which is which. If you make a mistake and get them switched, you can very easily pinch a finger. (And that does smart on a cold morning!) The best insurance against this that I've found is to hold the antlers in a way that both curve in the same direction; in other words, the front of one antler is beat against the back side of the other. Some old-timers use the antlers with tines facing, but this is a good way for a beginner to get a bruised thumb or forefinger. Sawing off the sharp tips of the tines makes the antlers safer to carry.

An easier way to simulate the real sound is to envision a buck fight. First they're squared off; then they run together, hit hard and begin twisting and trying to "throw" the other guy. If you can imagine that, you can come nearer to duplicating it than just hitting two antlers together at random.

Make your rattling sequence relatively short. In open country where you think a prolonged sound is required to give a buck's "direction finder" time to work, rattle the first sequence for about one minute. In close cover, I do half of that or less because I want to get the horns put down and the rifle in my hands in case a close buck comes sailing over the shrubbery.

There is a dangerous side to horn rattling, particularly in country where you don't know the location or identity of other hunters. A beginning hunter, seeing a couple of deer antlers moving in the brush may shoot first and ask questions afterward.

For that reason, I have for some years painted my rattling horns with fluorescent red paint. Deer are color blind, and if you're rattling properly, you'll be keeping the antlers low to the ground and behind brush so a buck can't see them anyway. The red color doesn't hurt your odds with deer; I believe it improves them with people.

In carrying the antlers from one location to the next, it is wise to keep them low. I often sling mine over my shoulder. (I keep them tied together at the base with a length of thong, tape or string.)

The first time any beginner tries horn rattling, he's apt to feel foolish. My suggestion is to start out alone—maybe practice a little at home to get the feel and mesh of the antlers. Then go out and try some patience and positive thinking.

The method isn't magic, but it's the most fascinating form of deer hunting I've found. And the first time a big buck comes charging up with the hair on his neck raised and eyes glaring, you may miss him, but you'll sure be hooked on the horns.

The Indestructible Wapiti

Jack O'Connor

Some very strange tales about the American wapiti or "elk" are going around these days. Those who are taken in by them are convinced that a bull elk is as tough as a Cape buffalo, and just about as dangerous.

One writer does not think elk can be taken consistently with anything less lethal than a cartridge using a .35-caliber bullet weighing 250 grains. This same man has saved his own life on a couple of occasions because he carried a six-shooter full of .45-caliber cartridges. When wounded elk charged him, he stood his ground and fought it out.

Recently a man on the editorial staff of an outdoor magazine wrote me that another outdoor writer, "a man of great integrity whose word he believed implicitly," had written him that he had shot a bull elk five times "through the lungs" with the 175-grain bullet of the 7 mm Remington Magnum before the elk finally went down.

Still another writer felt that the elk was so tough that a .50 caliber machine gun cartridge loaded with an expanding bullet would be about right. This man said that every elk season he saw many big bulls trotting around punctured fore, aft and amidship with .30/06 and .270 bullets, and leaking blood from a dozen holes. He said he would see the same bulls hours later, still leaking blood, still rattling from the bullets they carried, but not otherwise greatly bothered. The article was so silly that I wrote a letter of mild protest to the managing editor, who is a gifted guy and a friend of mine, but who has had about as much experience on big game as I had when I was thirteen. He replied with the trite old saw that he believed in using the biggest rifle he could handle because then, even if "you didn't place your shot well, you'd still get the game." I'll discuss this point later.

Another sport wrote that a companion of his had hit a bull elk with a 130-grain Silvertip .270 bullet in the middle of the neck as the elk faced him—in the spot where the adam's apple would be if elk had adam's apples. This elk was not knocked off its feet. Bleeding heavily, it ran over half a mile. It was climbing a hill when it fell and rolled, breaking down a few small trees. When found, it needed another shot.

I do not keep track of such things, but I would estimate that in six decades of hunting, I may have seen about 1000 head of game shot. Of these, maybe 50 were shot in the neck. I have never seen an animal hit solidly in the neck that did not drop. If the bullet is close to the neck vertebra or breaks it, the animal dies instantly. If the bullet is some distance away from the spine, the animal will generally fall, get up and move off. Often he will recover. In the pioneer days in the West, one way to catch wild mustangs was to "crease" them—to shoot them high in the neck to miss the spine. The horse dropped, and the hunter tied him up before he could recover.

Now the incident I relate above might have happened exactly as described, but I doubt it. It is about as believable as the tale I once heard about a man who drove an automobile a mile after his head was blown off. Whether the corpse stopped for traffic lights or not, I cannot remember.

I am reminded of a classic tale which appeared in a minor magazine's shooting department. The departmental editor, who was very pro-big bore, anti-.270, told how a pal of his had encountered a "small black bear" on a trail in the mountains. This chap lifted a .270 and drove a 130-grain bullet right in the bear's chest as it faced him at short range. The bear climbed a tree. Our boy pumped four more 130-grain .270 bullets into the bear's lungs. The bear stayed in the tree. A nearby hunter heard the commotion and came to the rescue with a .300 H. & H. Magnum. Another shot through the lungs with a 180-grain .30 caliber bullet did not seem to bother the bear, so the second guy shot the bear in the neck. At long last he fell out of the tree.

I wrote this editor, twitting him a bit and asking for particulars. He replied that it had happened *exactly* as he described it, and he added that he himself was a big game hunter of vast experience. Well, maybe so. . . .

People make up tales to prove a point. They make up tales to salve their egos after they have made a miss. Maybe they simply hunger for a new rifle, and want to convince themselves and their wives that bullets from the .30/06 bounce off an elk.

There are many more poor elk shots than there are poor elk calibers. I remember hearing a gun-nut friend lecture a hillbilly who had a peckerwood ranch on Arizona's Mogollon Rim. This man did odd jobs for the Forest Service, trapped and made moonshine that he sold for $4.00 a gallon. Every year he shot about six or eight elk to feed his family. All with a .30/30! Sometimes he shot them in the neck. More often he shot them in the lungs. He told me that often these lung-shot elk went down in their tracks, but generally they ran for 25 to 50 yards before they fell. He was rather apologetic about shooting elk with a .30/30 when he was told that was not the proper thing to do.

Elk are usually wounded, not because of the use of a cartridge that is too light, but because of poor shooting. If the hunter is going to gut-shoot an elk, clip it across the rump or break a leg, it doesn't make much difference what caliber he uses. An animal is just about as gut-shot when hit with a .458 as he is hit in the same place with a .243. Another cause of wounded game is the use of unsuitable or poorly designed bullets. Light, thin-jacketed varmint-type bullets should never be used on elk—the 110 and 125-grain bullets in the .30/06, the 100- to 110-grain bullets in the .270, etc. Today, just about all bullets designed for big game are very good. I have used Winchester-Western Silvertips and Power Points, Remington Core-Lokts, Noslers, Speers and Sierras. Some hold together a bit better; some expand a bit faster, but almost all will do the business!

In the past, that was not always true. One bullet was beautifully designed ballistically, but very unreliable on game. I had a couple of the bullets blow up on the ribs of a deer. The buck looked as if it had been killed with a shotgun. This same bullet made saucer-sized shallow holes in an elk's lungs. The elk got away and was later found. Even more curious, I once shot a large ram with bullets of the same design as it ran directly away. Both shots hit the left ham. One bullet went clear through and came out the brisket. The other came out behind the right shoulder. Neither had expanded at all.

Back in the 1920's and 1930's, some bullets expanded too slowly, some too fast. Some did well on light animals, some well on heavy animals. Today, most big-game bullets are of the "controlled expanding" type.

Many of our ideas of killing-power derive from the muzzle-loading days. When all bullets were of pure lead and were driven

Many bulls are bugled up in heavy timber where the hunter can't get a decent shot until they are within a few yards. Even then he may be able to see only a small part of a bull that is not in an ideal position for perfect bullet placement. It is better to have more gun than you need than not enough. Heavy, deep penetrating bullets of fairly large caliber from cartridges that pack plenty of punch are the answer to sure kills.

by black powder, about the only way killing-power could be increased was by making the bullet of larger caliber, and consequently heavier. In black-powder days, a .50 caliber was almost a small bore. The Dutch in South Africa shot elephants with 4-bores using bullets that weighed a quarter of a pound. Sir Samuel Baker, the African hunter and explorer, had an elephant gun that was a 2-bore, using explosive bullets weighing one-half pound.

An elk is, compared to a deer, a pretty large animal. It takes a very big deer to dress out 45 pounds to the quarter. Elk are often killed that dress out three times that. I have not weighed many elk quarters, but I have weighed some. The first bull I ever shot, a large five-pointer, weighed 115 pounds to the quarter. He was shot in Arizona toward the end of November. He had been through the rut and was as lean as a greyhound. Another elk I weighed went 125 pounds to the quarter. I have heard of one bull that dressed out 150 pounds to the quarter.

The rib cage of an elk is thicker than that of a deer, and the bones are heavier. An elk has more meat on his carcass. All this means that the elk hunter should use a stoutly constructed bullet that will expand inside the animal. The thin-jacket bullets with soft cores that blow varmints sky high, and often give spectacular results on deer, are not suitable for elk. A friend of mine went elk hunting with a .25/06. He used a 100-grain bullet of the varmint-type, driven along at around 3400 feet per second.

He and his guide heard a bull bugling in the bottom of a deep canyon. They tied their horses on a ridge and went down. My pal put four varmint-type bullets (he said) into the bull's shoulder, and every one of them blew up on the shoulder blade. He had left his spare cartridges on his horse. He and the guide decided to come back the next day and get the wounded elk. During the night it snowed heavily, and the hunters had to pack out. The next spring, the guide went back and found the remains of the elk. He sent my friend the antlers. The bull was a fine six-pointer.

Some might say that the moral of this tale is that for elk hunting, the hunter needs a rifle of large bore and a heavy bullet. I think it shows two things—the necessity of using a well-constructed bullet, and the foolishness of using the shoulder shot on non-dangerous game. There is always the possibility that a fairly light bullet will go to pieces on heavy bone, and there is nothing to be gained by aiming at the shoulder blade. A fairly heavy bullet on the shoulder blade will knock down and disable a grizzly bear, a lion or a tiger, It will also knock down an elk or a moose, but it will also shoot up a lot of edible meat.

Instead, the place to put the bullet is in the lungs. If it expands and gets inside, it is a physiological impossibility for the animal to live long. He will drown in his own blood in minutes, if not in seconds. I read touching tales of elk hit with solid lung shots with bullets of .270, 7 mm and .30 caliber running all over the place. Don't you believe it! When you read those stories someone is pulling your leg!

Unless I have to take a crack at an animal's neck when he stands with his body concealed behind a tree, I always aim for the lungs. Good advice is to aim so as to break the shoulder blade or the upper leg bone on the opposite side.

An elk wounded by a companion was quartering away in an open basin at about 250 yards. I tried to put the bullet behind the last rib on the left side, so it would range forward toward the right shoulder. When I shot, the bull took three or four more steps, stopped and fell over. I used a 150-grain Nosler bullet in a .270. I took my first bull moose with a shot about identical. I used a 130-grain Silvertip in a .270. It was at about thirty yards. My best greater kudu (an elk-size African antelope) was likewise quartering away at short range and a .30/06 180-grain Core-Lokt bullet drove up through his abdomen into his right lung. He went about 300 yards.

I have passed up chances to shoot elk in the buttocks. I have heard of expanding bullets that would drive through an elk's ham, up through intestines and paunch and into the lungs. A full metal-jacketed round-nose solid would probably do it, but I do not think any soft point will. In 1959 I gut-shot a large eland on the Kilombero River of Tanzania. As it ran across an open plain directly away from me, I lobbed five .375 300-grain Western Silvertip bullets into its bottom. These slowed him up but did not kill him. My professional hunter sprinted ahead, drew even with the bull and killed the bull with a lung shot from a .243 Winchester.

The old saw about using the most powerful rifle you can carry so if you do not place the shot right, you'll still get the game, is absurd. I have seen too many animals wounded with too many different calibers not to know baloney when I hear it. People shoot at elk at too great a distance. They shoot from unsteady, insecure positions. They shoot when they can only see a patch of tan hide, and do not know what part of the animal they are

Most ''elk rubs'' are made during the rut when the bulls are bugling. This bull skinned the sapling up to seven feet. This doesn't mean he was necessarily a record class bull, but he sure wasn't a spike!

shooting at. One of the differences between a good game shot and a poor one is that the good game shot knows when to shoot. The good game shot doesn't fire unless he is reasonably certain just where his bullet will land. The excitable, inexperienced shot bangs away at the first opportunity—and hopes. Then if he misses or wounds, he blames his rifle, the choice of bullet or something else.

I read that hunting pressure has changed the habits of elk and that they are now brush-dwelling animals to a much greater extent than they used to be. This may be so in some areas. In the parts of the Idaho elk country with which I am familiar, elk have lived in the brush for the last thirty years. Along Arizona's Mogollon Rim in the 1930's, elk were often found in fairly open yellow pine and fir country, but mostly they were in pretty thick stuff. The Colorado elk I have seen have been in brushy country, and so have those in Alberta. I have seen many elk in beautiful open basins above timberline in Wyoming. However, I have not hunted elk in Wyoming for about ten years. My experience is limited, and I may be wrong, but it has struck me that elk are not nearly as hard to sneak up on in the brush as moose and deer. An interesting habit that bull elk have is to stand on a steep hill in a little opening like torch singers in a spotlight surveying the country. When a big six-pointer does that, he is a grand sight.

Les Bowman was a guide, outfitter and gun-nut in Wyoming for a good many years. He tells me that he has seen more elk wounded and lost with the super .300 Magnums than with anything else. This is not to say that such cartridges as the .300 Winchester Magnum, the .308 Norma and the .300 Weatherby are not good cartridges, as they are. Many of the hunters who show up with them have done little hunting, don't have their rifles properly sighted in, and haven't shot them enough to be familiar with them. They are afraid of them, flinch and shoot poorly. (Les sees no point in dragging around a 9- to 9½ pound .375 or even slightly lighter .338, and is partial to the 7 mm Remington Magnum).

I have had two 7 mm Remington Magnums—one a Remington Model 700, and the other a very fancy custom job on a pre-1964 Winchester Model 70 action. I have shot elk in the United States with the 7 mm Magnum, chital (spotted axis deer) and nilgai (blue bull, a large heavy antelope) in India, and kudu, sable, zebra and other African animals the size of elk on safaris in Mozambique and Angola. With the Remington factory-load and the 150-grain pointed soft-point Core-Lokt bullet, I found the 7 mm Remington Magnum very deadly on anything I pointed it at. The best Idaho elk I have ever taken was killed in its tracks with one shot. This bull was 100–125 yards away, and was struck with the 150-grain Remington Core-Lokt bullet.

Nevertheless, I prefer the .270 or the .280, and here are the reasons. To get markedly higher velocity with the 7 mm Magnum as compared to the two milder cartridges, at least a 24-inch barrel is needed. A 26-inch is better. The rifle for the Magnum cartridge should be heavier if the recoil is not to be unpleasant. I have found that a 9-pound 7 mm Magnum kicks about the same as an 8-pound .270 or .280. I do not consider magazine capacity terribly important, but the time might arise when the fact that a magazine will hold more .270 or .280 cartridges than 7 mm Magnums is important.

Much elk hunting consists of scrambling around on steep, rough hillsides in thick brush. For work like that, I prefer a light rifle with a fairly short barrel—not over 22 inches. It is all very nice to say that the elk hunter should undergo a rigorous course of training until he can pack around a 10-pound rifle and bulldoze down the brush with brute strength. This will not happen.

The .30/06 is a fine elk cartridge, and in modern times it has probably killed more elk than any other. A friend of mine who has taken many elk swears by the 150-grain .30/06 bullet. For no particular reason, I prefer the 180, just as I generally use the 150-grain bullet in the .270.

In Idaho, the elk country with which I am most familiar, the hills are high, very steep and generally brushy. Shots are generally short if the elk is on the same side of the hill as the hunter. If the elk is across the canyon, the shot will be from 200 to 400 yards. For this reason, the elk rifle should have a fairly flat trajectory, and the hunter should know the bullet drop at 300 and 400 yards. In Idaho, I have shot elk at less than 100 yards and more than 300.

Some believers in mighty elk rifles will fall into a swoon at this, but used with skill and discretion, the .257 Roberts and the 7 x 57 Mauser are both adequate elk cartridges. A physician friend of mine, who is now dead, was a crack varmint shot. He told me he had used a .257 Roberts with the 100-grain bullet on about thirty elk, and had never lost one. On an extended hunting trip from Alaska to Nevada, Prince Abdorreza Pahlavi of Iran used a 7 x 57. He got his Wyoming elk with one well-placed 140-grain bullet. My wife has shot elk and all kinds of large African antelope with a 7 x 57.

The point of all this is, I repeat, that there are a lot more inadequate elk hunters than inadequate elk cartridges. If anyone enjoys lugging around a .357 Magnum with a 25-inch barrel and weighing ten pounds, I am all for him. If striding forth into the forest clutching some monster Magnum that lays the daisies low for miles around gives him joy, again I am for him. If clutching a potent Super .300 blaster fills him full of euphoria, once more I rejoice.

But what bugs me is to have someone come up to me, fix me with his glittering eye, and tell me that only very powerful cartridges with large-caliber, heavy bullets should be used when hunting elk.

That simply is not so. A good shot with patience and judgment is well-armed with about any big game cartridge from a .30/ 30 up. The poor shot, the excitable man, the person without judgment would be inadequately armed with a .416 Rigby. The ideal rifle for anyone is the rifle the hunter knows, has shot a lot, has killed game with, and in which he has perfect confidence!

Hunting Dangerous Game

Elgin T. Gates

Four hours ago, my Canadian guide Roy Hensen and I had tied the boat to a driftwood log a mile down river, and cautiously followed the deeply-embedded bear trail that led along the bank to the riffle. Less than 100 yards from our position, a grizzly sow and her two cubs were trying to catch darting salmon. Fresh tracks were everywhere, solid proof that this was one of the favorite hangouts of the giant coastal grizzlies during the annual fall salmon runs.

I had hunted most of the species of grizzlies from the dark brown grizzlies of Montana to the beautiful long-haired barren-ground grizzlies that are found north of the Arctic circle in Alaska. As a confirmed trophy hunter, I had known for a long time that the top-ranking grizzly trophies had been taken along the inlets and rivers that drain the coastal mountains of British Columbia. My final choice for this hunt was the Klina Klini river that flows into the Knight inlet about 200 miles northwest of Vancouver.

Several years back, I had completed a grand slam of all four bears—the grizzly, polar, brown and black. All of them ranked in the record book, although the grizzly was near the bottom of the list. When the minimum qualifying score was raised, my grizzly was dropped, so the prime purpose of this trip was to collect a grizzly that would give me a record book grand slam again.

Hensen put one hand on my shoulder. "We've got more company," he whispered.

At the head of the riffle, another sow, this one with three cubs, had come out of the dense alders along the bank and was testing the wind with her outstretched nose as the cubs gamboled at the edge of the water.

A few minutes later, a huge, shaggy bear came into sight from below. He walked with a slight limp, favoring his right front paw.

Hensen recognized the bear instantly. "That's him," he whispered, "the one that killed those two fishermen. Shoot as soon as you get a chance. If he gets our wind, or if one of those sows get too close, there will be hell to pay."

As Hensen spoke, I could feel the hackles rise on the back of my neck, and a swift surge of adrenaline tingled in my veins. It always happens that way, any time I get in close proximity to dangerous game. The reaction came swiftly this time, for the details of the chilling story Hensen had told me the night before were still fresh in mind. About nine months back, a party of four men in two canoes had made a trip down river, fishing and camping along the way. One of the canoes came around a bend near the bank and ran onto the big grizzly. He promptly attacked, smashing the canoe to splinters, and killing both men while their companions could only look on in horror from the other canoe. The only weapon they had was a .22 pistol, which they emptied at the bear, only further enraging him. Only the fact that the second canoe was farther out in the river in deeper water saved them from the same fate.

Hensen told me a party was organized to track down the killer grizzly, but the hunt was unsuccessful. Subsequently, everyone visiting this part of the coast was told the story, and warned to be extremely careful.

It may be one kind of danger to inch along a narrow, snow-slicked ledge in the high country while stalking a wily ram, or picking your way through a treacherous moraine of glacial ice after a record-class white goat. I've had many of these experiences. But nothing in hunting equals the thrill of a head-on confrontation with a dangerous big game animal.

In Africa and Asia, there is a long list of animals in this category, including the Big Five of Africa—namely the elephant, rhino, Cape buffalo, lion and leopard. Asia has elephants, water buffaloes, gaur, tiger, panthers and others. I've faced all of them at one time or another.

The list for the Western Hemisphere is rather short. At the top is the grizzly bear, easily the most dangerous big game animal in North America by a country mile.

During forty years of hunting dangerous game all over the world, I've arrived at one firm conviction. Don't be undergunned! While it is true that men have taken every animal in the world (including elephants) with some of the old tried-and-true calibers, such as the 30-30, .30/06 and .270, I wouldn't want to use anything less potent than one of the medium magnums in .30 to .35 caliber for grizzly and other dangerous game of that size. My favorite rifle in this class is a .300 Weatherby magnum with a 2X-7X variable scope, using 200-grain Nosler partition bullets for the larger animals at close range. I use the Nosler because my preferred aiming spot is the point of the shoulder. The idea is to break bone, and plenty of it. A well-placed bullet at this point, if not an instant kill, will penetrate through and break the off shoulder, which will always anchor the trophy. Any dangerous animal with one or both front shoulders broken won't be charging the hunter. A hit that is a little high will catch the spine for an instant kill. If the bullet is a bit back, it will be a lung or heart shot.

Actually, for a feeling of security, one of the larger magnums, such as the .375 or the .458 Winchester, is potent medicine for the big bears because of the greater shock and stopping power.

The point is: One mistake with a dangerous animal may be your last. The wrong rifle, the wrong cartridge, the wrong placement or the wrong bullet has ended a number of hunting careers permanently.

The literature of hunting is full of legends about man-killing grizzlies from the earliest days of western exploration in America. Lewis and Clark wrote that they would rather face Indians than grizzly bears, and the trappers and mountain men of the 1820's and 1830's, knowing their small-bore Kentucky rifles were no match for an enraged grizzly, avoided the huge bears whenever possible. One of the most notable feats among the Plains Indians was to kill a grizzly in a head-on confrontation. With only a bow and arrow, and possibly a lance, it was a feat that brought the warrior lasting renown in his tribe.

What makes the grizzly dangerous?

Virtually all grizzly attacks result from one of three situations: a sow who thinks her cubs are endangered when someone accidentally stumbles onto the scene; wounding a bear and being careless in following it up; and encountering a grizzly on a kill.

Prince Abdorreza Pahlavi, one of the world's top trophy hunters, with a beautiful silvertip grizzly bagged in Alaska on a hunting trip with author.

On many occasions, a hunter has shot a moose, caribou or some other trophy, then came back to the carcass a day or so later to find that a grizzly has taken possession. One unlucky fellow and his guide came back to a moose carcass to look for a skinning knife, never dreaming they were walking into an ambush. An enraged grizzly came roaring out of a nearby thicket where he was lying up after feasting on the moose, and killed the hunter and severely mauled the guide.

Occasionally, a grizzly will attack unprovoked. Even then it may be instigated by an old bullet wound, or by a battle-scarred old bear who has been in too many fights and is on the prod.

Hardly a year goes by without a reported killing or maiming of someone by a grizzly, ranging from the backpacker who was mauled in a national park to the unwary hunter who just happened to be in the wrong place at the wrong time.

A few years ago, a fellow who had pulled off the dubious stunt of bagging one each of the four North American species of sheep in one season went on a fishing trip with a guide and another companion in Alberta's Jasper National Park. They became involved in another kind of stunt that vividly demonstrates the terrible ferocity of a grizzly.

While on the trail, they encountered a grizzly sow with two cubs. She first severely mauled the guide who was in the lead. The sheep-hunter scrambled up a tree, and then made the mistake of yelling. In a flash, the grizzly came running, and went up the tree like a squirrel. Grabbing the man by the leg with her teeth, she hauled him down and worked him over savagely. The third man arrived on the scene and promptly was attacked by the enraged sow. Then she went off after her cubs.

The whole affair lasted about six or seven minutes. By a miracle, all three men lived, but they remain scarred and crippled to this day.

These men were unarmed except for pocket knives. Had one of them had a handgun, the horrible consequences possibly could have been avoided.

It has been my habit over the years to carry a 4-inch S&W .357 magnum during stalks after dangerous game. I've never been mauled by any wild beast yet. Mainly, I believe, because of my refusal to fire unless I can get a first well-aimed shot at a vital area. On the other hand, I've been treed by a berserk Cape buffalo, and killed him with the .357 at about thirty feet with a slug between the eyes. On another occasion, I had to shoot an African lion off of a hunting companion at fifteen feet.

Grizzly sow and her two cubs at the edge of a river during the salmon run. The most dangerous situation anyone can get into is to accidentally get between a grizzly and her cubs.

He had gut-shot the lion with a .470 double rifle, necessitating a follow-up stalk in fairly dense brush.

When a dangerous animal comes for you at close range, for whatever the reason, you don't have time to choose and pick the exact place to put a bullet. You try for a frontal brain shot if there is time, otherwise the idea is to put a slug into the animal, and more than one if possible.

During one memorable trip to Alaska, I was hunting with Prince Abdorreza Pahlavi, brother of the Shah of Iran. The Prince is one of the world's great trophy hunters. On a previous trip to Iran as his guest, during which I collected an excellent bag of Persian trophies, we had discussed his forthcoming trip to North America. The Prince is a confirmed sheep hunter, but above all else, he wanted a grizzly bear. He had read many of the grizzly legends and had a preconceived, but healthy, respect for the animal.

As part of the Prince's hunt was to collect specimens for the national museum in Tehran, he had a special permit for a second grizzly bear.

His first grizzly was a piece of cake. We had been stalking moose in the Talkeetna mountains, and ran across a beautiful silvertip that he dropped with one shot from his 7mm magnum using a 172-grain bullet. It was so easy, I had a feeling the Prince may have thought some of the grizzly tales he had read were a bit exaggerated.

The next encounter dispelled that notion. The Prince had taken a fine record-class moose a day or two before his first grizzly. Several days later, passing near the remains, we saw that a huge boar grizzly had taken possession of the carcass, and was sprawled out on top of it. After a short stalk to the top of a small hill nearby, the Prince fired from a sitting position. The bullet struck home, but only wounded the bear. What happened next was at once hilarious and terrifying. Not knowing where the shot came from, and thinking the moose carcass was somehow responsible for his hurt, the big boar went absolutely berserk. He attacked the carcass with fanatical fury, literally dismembering it with mighty blows from his sickle-clawed paws and violent wrenches from his huge jaws.

We sat there in virtual shock for several minutes watching his furious assault until he began to slow down, and the Prince put in a clincher shot. Needless to say, we approached this grizzly with extraordinary caution.

Next to a grizzly in danger, insofar as the number of recorded attacks on humans, is the brown bear of Kodiak and the Alaskan peninsula. The big brownies do not have the aggressive instincts of the grizzlies.

The Alaskan brown bear has many reputations. To most big game hunters, he is one of the finest trophies in North America. To other people, he is a shy, benign creature who minds his own business, harming no one. To still others, he is an evil beast of hair-trigger temperament who, like a grizzly, will wait silently to pounce on a chosen victim, or come charging out of the dense alders in a tooth-chomping rage—with the toughness to absorb bullet after bullet from a high-powered rifle, and still come to

Glassing the coastal country of British Columbia for grizzly bears. They come down from the mountains to catch salmon in the creeks and rivers, and this is the best chance the hunter has of finding them in the open.

grips with his antagonist. Hardly a year goes by in Alaska without a guide or client getting killed or maimed by a brown bear.

As with the grizzly, a brown bear sow with cubs is the most dangerous. Next is a battle-hardened old boar with, perhaps, a festering wound from a recent fight, or an old injury that never completely healed. A wounded brownie can be extremely dangerous, especially when you have to go into heavy cover after him. A man doesn't stand a chance in a patch of alders. He can't run, but an enraged bear can smash through the brush with ease.

One of the most vivid memories I have of a big game hunt is a long grueling stalk that brought me face to face with a great Alaskan brown bear.

Early that morning, my guide and I had climbed high up on the snowy slopes of Mount Veniaminof, far out on the Alaskan peninsula, to spy the country with binoculars and spotting scopes. Salmon were still running, and the bears were down on the creeks gorging themselves. From our vantage-point, we spotted fifty-seven bears. Many of them were females with cubs, but at least a dozen were big, hulking boars, several of which were in the ten-foot class. On these we concentrated our attention, trying to select the largest. I finally decided on a shaggy monster that stood a little higher than the others, and we began the stalk.

Brown bears are reputed to have poor eyesight, but ultra-sensitive senses of smell and hearing. This big boar must have heard us, in spite of the care of our stalk, and suddenly he reared up less than fifty feet away. He stood there in regal majesty, nose twitching, mighty paws half raised, his face bloody from the fresh salmon he was eating.

In the two or three seconds it took to raise my .458 Winchester, I remembered something else I had heard, that brown bears—like many other animals—are more likely to attack when their feeding is interrupted.

I brought him down with a clean shot through the neck, not waiting to see if he would take off or take us.

Probably just as dangerous as the brownie, possibly even more so, is the polar bear. But due to the peculiar circumstances

Polar bear taken on the Arctic ice pack of the Bering Sea, west of Kotsebut, Alaska. This bear had identified the seal skin parka and clothing worn by Gates as its natural prey.

of its habitat in the arctic regions of the far north, and minimum contact with mankind, the real answer will never be known.

Polar bears live mainly on seals, which they catch by lying in wait at their breathing holes in the ice; but they will eat anything else they find on the ice pack, living or dead.

The polar bear has no natural enemies, and has never learned to fear man. Consequently, he will come to investigate any strange thing he encounters on the ice pack with the presumption it will be edible.

Long ago, Eskimos hunted them with dog sleds, then big game hunters began flying out over the ice with light planes. The Arctic is unforgiving, and more hunters and guides were killed by crashing on the ice, and from exposure to the terrible Arctic weather, than from polar bear attacks. Nevertheless, a close confrontation with a polar bear can be a vivid and long-remembered experience.

Few wild animals I've ever faced affected me as much as a great white polar bear I encountered during one memorable hunt north of the Arctic Circle. I rounded a broken pressure ridge and met him almost head on coming my way. He was less than forty yards from where I stood. He saw me instantly, but never paused. As he was downwind, my scent must have been filling his nose, but he came on through the snow, his big head wagging from side to side.

It was not a charge in any sense of the word. The bear probably had never seen a man before, and was totally unafraid. I had an eerie feeling that if I turned to run in my clumsy mukluks and heavy seal skin pants and parka, he could easily overhaul me. Later, I realized he had recognized my seal skin clothes as familiar prey, and simply was coming after them.

It seemed an eternity as I fought to get the big heavy mitten off my right hand so I could raise my rifle and reach for the trigger. He cut the distance to twenty-five yards while I wrestled with the frozen safety. Exerting every ounce of strength I had in desperation, it finally moved. I vividly remember wondering if the firing pin also would be frozen in position as I brought the rifle up. It fired, and the bullet went true. The final distance, sixteen paces.

The fourth member of the bear family, the North American black bear, is generally a shy, cowardly beast that has little rating insofar as being considered dangerous. Black bear attacks are rare, although there are a few known instances where men have been killed by them.

Terrain along the rugged Alaskan Peninsula is the habitat of the brown bear, largest carniverous land animal in the world. It is considered one of North America's finest big game trophies, and second only to the grizzly in the category of dangerous animals.

Other than the three biggest bears, the grizzly, brown and polar, it is difficult to come up with any other North American animal that could be considered aggressively dangerous.

To be sure, if you read everything that has been written about hunting, you will find accounts where somebody has been killed or wounded by virtually every big game animal in North America.

Not long ago, I read where a man was accidently killed by a whitetail deer. It seems he had shot the buck, leaned his rifle against a nearby tree, then straddled the animal to cut its throat, thinking it was dead. At the touch of the knife, the buck reared up, and in so doing, caught the man on his antlers, driving one tine through the hunter's neck.

An animal as large as a moose can be dangerous, especially during the rut. There are a number of authenticated accounts of men being killed by moose.

Several years ago I saw a photograph of the bones of a moose and a trapper mixed together. From the evidence on the scene, including the battered rifle of the trapper—which had an empty shell in the chamber—it appeared that the moose had been shot, but had enough strength left to kill the trapper when he arrived on the scene.

On occasion, men have been killed by wounded jaguars. One of the Lee brothers, famous cat-hunters from Tucson, Arizona, once told me that years back there was a man-eating jaguar on the west coast of Mexico. The cat killed ten or twelve people before it was tracked down with dogs and was shot.

Even the lowly javelina gets credit for an attack now and then. One account from Arizona had it that a hunter followed a wounded javelina into a cave, crawling on hands and knees after it, flashlight in one hand, a six-gun in the other. Spotting the beast at the rear of the cave, he blasted away, dropping his flashlight in the process. In the melee that followed, the man got slashed about the face, and came home with a thrilling tale about how dangerous a charging javelina can be. In simple truth, the poor pig probably was doing his best to get away, and ran into the man while on his way out of the cave.

The point is, any big game animal has the potential of being dangerous under certain circumstances, especially a mother protecting her young. A wise hunter who wants to live to a ripe old age should always be alert and cautious any time he is in hunting country, and be ready for instant action. It is usually the unexpected that is most dangerous.

The nearest brush with disaster I've ever had while hunting in North America was with a female grizzly, and the whole affair was an unexpected accident.

The occasion was during a pack trip into the Yukon on a sheep hunt. On the second day, the strap of my rifle scabbard caught on a dead limb and broke. Since it was only a few more miles to camp, I slung the rifle over my shoulder. It was a simple act, but one that possibly saved my life. About fifteen minutes later, we rounded a point, and by a stroke of bad luck happened to get between a grizzly and her cubs. Several things happened

The killer grizzly where he fell on the bank of the Klina Klini river in British Columbia. This bear had killed two fishermen a few months previously. The cause of his savage disposition was an old bullet wound.

in short order. One of the cubs bawled at the same time as the lead pack horse got a nose full of bear scent. If there is one thing a horse is absolutely terrified of it is a bear. In that same brief interlude before all hell broke loose, I heard the raging, deep-throated growl of the sow from the brush just to the right of the trail, followed by the spine-chilling sound of her fangs chomping together like castanets. The horses went crazy, scattering their loads and riders in all directions. I stayed on for four or five bucks as my horse cut to the left away from the grizzly, then the next thing I remember, I was sprawled out on the ground, flat on my stomach, partly stunned from the fall. Back on the trail, the sow had caught one of the horses that was close to her, and felled it with a blow of her paw. She savaged it with several bites, and when the horse no longer moved, she began to look around.

By that time, I had managed to sit up and bring the rifle—which still was on my back with the sling across my chest—over my head and down to where I could change a cartridge. In hunting country, I always keep the magazine full, but nothing in the chamber while riding a horse. The bear heard the sound of the bolt going in and spotted me just as I raised the rifle, still in a sitting position. I'll always think the goddess of the hunt had a hand in this affair, because in addition to the broken scabbard strap which caused me to carry the rifle, the variable scope was at its minimum setting of 2X. Why? I could never remember, for in sheep country, long shots are the rule, and it would have been natural for me to leave the scope at its maximum magnification. The point is, at 7X, with the bear less than forty yards away, I'd have seen nothing but hair, and wouldn't have known where I was aiming. At 2X I could see the head of the enraged sow. As she started my way, I fired instinctively, and had my third piece of luck in fifteen minutes when the 180-grain Hornady soft-point hit just over the grizzly's left eye for an instant kill.

I walked the rest of the way to camp in sober thought, at the same time grateful for the series of coincidences that saved me from a certain, possibly fatal, mauling.

It was this very incident I was thinking about as Roy Hensen and I began to ease out from under the fallen tree that was our shelter on the Klina Klini river. Just ahead, at the very edge of the bank, was a low clump of brush and a hummock covered with dry grass, from which I would have a clear shot.

But things began to move more rapidly than we anticipated. The killer grizzly suddenly got our wind, and came churning through the shallow water with the head-swinging, shoulder-rolling stride that is characteristic of big bears. He let out a roar of rage. The startled sow, unaware of his presence until now, bawled at the cubs, and headed flat-out for the bank in our direction.

Both Hensen and I instantly recognized the potential danger that was at hand. If she held her line, she would hit the bank a short distance below us if the big boar, coming from a different angle, didn't change her mind.

I'd already chambered a cartridge in my .300 Weatherby magnum, and now rose to a kneeling position to get a clear shot. The big boar was coming hard, about fifty yards out. Just as I leveled the rifle, the sow crossed in front, spraying water in all directions. I don't think she ever knew we were there. The boar ignored her, his whole attention fixed on us. I put the cross hairs on his chest and fired. The bullet knocked him flat, and a sheet of water spurted high. He was up before I could chamber another cartridge, and came on, momentarily shielded by the bank in front of us.

The plunging sow was now at the bank, her terrified cubs right on her heels. Everything seemed to be happening in a dreamy, slow-motion type of action that medical men have told me is the result of ones whole system being hyped-up with adrenaline.

As the big boar came over the bank, he stumbled and fell on his side. As he came up again, I had a clear side shot, and put in another 200-grain Nosler, this time on the point of his shoulder. He took two or three more lurching steps, and went down hard. This time he didn't get up.

Much later, after our adrenaline-charged nerves had calmed down, we commenced the laborious job of skinning. I was anxious to examine his lame paw, to see what had turned him into a killer. What we found was an old .30-caliber jacketed bullet that had fragmented and broken the first joint of his foot, leaving him with a permanent limp.

"Probably from some commercial salmon fisherman with a 30-30." Hensen said, lighting up his pipe. "They take pot shots at every bear they see."

As he spoke, I was again thinking about that long-ago encounter with the enraged sow. I'd used up a lot of "bear luck" that time, even if the whole affair had been accidental. This time I had been lucky again. Here was a grizzly that would rank well in the book, and a trophy that anyone would be satisfied with. Twice now I had come out on the best end of a close confrontation with North America's most dangerous big-game animal. Maybe a third time would be one too many.

Rim-fire Rifles and Small Game

Jim Carmichel

Back when I was a farm lad in bib overalls and high-top shoes, the single-shot .22 rifle that hung on two pegs over the kitchen door was as much a part of everyday life as splitting stove-wood, milking the family's brindled cow and having corn dodgers and buttermilk for supper. And when I emptied my pockets on wash-day, there were always a half dozen or more .22 shells mixed among the nails, bolts, marbles and other essentials of rural boyhood.

The point I'm making is that the .22 rifle was always *there*. Whenever rats got in the corn crib or skunks got in the hen house, Dad would simply say: "Get the rifle." We had other guns of course, a couple of center-fire deer rifles and two or three shotguns, but the .22 was *the* rifle. It was a tool.

To a little boy like myself, it was also a source of endless fascination and mystery. And in my case, more than a little aggravation. Our .22 was a single-shot model with a slick, chrome-plated cocking knob. The striker spring must have been as stiff as a truck spring because of how difficult it was to cock. At age ten, I was big for my age, and stout enough to shoulder a sack of corn, but I still couldn't muster enough strength to pull that slippery knob to full cock. So I carried a pair of pliers to help with the chore.

When the pliers weren't handy, I could cock the thing by pulling with *both* hands. To do this, I would place the rifle, muzzle down, on a hard surface, then lean down on the butt like a crutch. With the rifle thus held in place, both hands were free to tug at the cocking knob. One summer day, I was employing this technique while standing on a large limestone outcropping. To make sure the muzzle didn't slip on the rock, I held it between my toes. That day my grip wasn't very sure, and the knob slipped from my grasp just before the sear caught. The rifle fired, and the bullet splatted between my bare toes, peppering them with lead and stone fragments. I yelped and danced around for some while before noticing that my toes were intact and, in fact, unharmed.

Another time when I was hunting in a thicket behind our back pasture, I spotted a rabbit sitting in a clump of sassafras saplings. To a boy used to potting rats and starlings, a rabbit was really *big* game. The rabbit was sitting perfectly still only a few feet away, so it wasn't likely I could miss. But I got excited and couldn't get the rifle cocked. I ran about a half mile to the nearest house and beseeched a startled housewife to help me cock the thing. It took a bit of explaining before she agreed to help out, and by the time I was back to the thicket, the rabbit was gone. Years later, when I inherited this rifle, I immediately traded it for a self-cocking repeater, and life has been much more agreeable ever since.

Now that I think back on it, I realize that the aggravations of that first rifle may very well have been a blessing in disguise. Since I went through so much misery getting it cocked, each shot was carefully planned, and as precisely aimed as the coarse sights would permit. Every missed shot called for an investigation of sorts, and some interesting discoveries were made. For example, I soon learned that it was not smart to shoot at a squirrel perched on the top side of a large limb because the bullet might pass cleanly through the squirrel, killing it instantly, but *not* knocking it off the limb. With a little experimenting I found that this was more likely to happen when using high speed, long rifle shells. Hollow point shorts, on the other hand, that did not zip through a squirrel so easily, seemed to "push" it off a limb more reliably.

Of course I soon came face to face with the mysteries and realities of trajectory. The owner of the neighboring farm had an eighty-acre alfalfa field which, in his opinion, was the showpiece of our entire community. In fact, he loved this hayfield so much that nearly every evening after supper he'd go there just to admire its gentle colors and contours in the sun's final rays. If so much as a rabbit dared to violate the field's rich greenness, he'd whoop like a madman, and chase it into the next county.

The only flaw he, or anyone else, could find with the alfalfa field was a grizzled old groundhog that had dug a maze of dens almost dead center in the field on a low knoll. The old groundhog had lived there for several seasons, and the landowner hated it like sin. Every effort to remove him had been futile, and the farmer passed the word that he would pay five dollars to anyone who could produce the carcass at his doorstep. Considering that a man's wage for a full working day was seldom more than five dollars in those parts, the bounty offer was more than tempting. A box of .22 shells cost thirty three cents in that era, and I'd never been able to afford more than one box at a time. With the five dollar bounty in hand, I reckoned that I'd be able to buy a whole carton of .22 ammo, and have a lot of walking around money left over.

The problem was that the old groundhog had been chased and shot at by every man, boy and dog in the community, and knew every trick in the book. From his lookout point on the knoll, he had a clear view of the surrounding area, and it was impossible to get closer than a hundred yards or so without him ducking into a hole. A modern day varmint rifle would have dispatched him with ease, but such wonders were unknown in our rural community.

The first morning I tried for the woodchuck, I settled myself in a sparse hedge on one end of the alfalfa field, and rested the rifle alongside a fencepost. I figured this was a pretty scientific form of sharpshooting—certainly more productive than the random sniping to which the chuck had been previously subjected—and that I'd have the five dollars before noon.

I hadn't waited more than a quarter hour before the old warrior came out and stood up on his haunches surveying his surroundings, and no doubt planning on eating a good portion of the lush alfalfa. The distance was the longest I'd ever attempted with any gun, and I estimated that the bullet would fall perhaps an inch or two before it got to the target. After all, the cartridge box said "Danger-Range One Mile" so, like everyone I knew, I assumed that the slug traveled nearly as straight as a string over much of that distance. So I estimated that if I held on his head, the bullet would hit him neatly in the heart. Such innocence.

But as soon as I leveled the sights on the standing target,

Here is my son, Eric, with a Franchi rimfire autoloader and a couple of grey squirrels. The rimfire rifle, a hickory tree and the squirrel, is, to my way of thinking, the essence of rimfire hunting.

Here's a picture of a happy hunter coming home with a couple of squirrels.

things started getting more complicated than I had anticipated. For one thing, the large front bead all but obscured the target. Thus, a precisely aimed shot, even if I had been capable of such a feat, was impossible. Still undaunted, I centered the bead in the rear notch, held where I figured his head ought to be, and pulled the trigger. After what seemed an amazingly long time, I saw a puff of dust several feet short of the target, and in an instant, the chuck was gone.

Two factors immediately became evident: first, the .22 bullet dropped a lot more than I had anticipated; and second, I

Here is a deluxe-grade Winchester Model 63 autoloader. These guns are no longer made, and have some pretty fancy prices on the used-gun market. A deluxe grade, such as this one from my collection, would be worth a lot of money. Actually, I would like to see more high-grade rimfire rifles than there are on the market today. If I'm going to hunt, I want to hunt with something really elegant, and I think a lot of other shooters feel the same way.

would have to devise a way of determining how much the bullet would fall at that distance, and adjust the sights accordingly.

Thinking myself pretty smart, I paced off the distance from the hedgerow to the chuck's redoubt. As I recall, it was about 120 of my youthful paces, which probably equalled something like 100 yards. Back at our place, I paced off a like distance and put up a target. The first shot, to my amazement, hit about two feet low. This was far more drop than I had imagined, but at least I was beginning to learn something about trajectory.

The rear sight had a simple elevator slide with a series of notches, and I tried raising it a notch at a time and rechecking the point of import. But as it turned out, the elevation slide did not raise the sight enough to get the point of impact on target at the necessary range. This was remedied by shimming with a sliver of cardboard or two.

A couple of days later, I tried to bag the old woodchuck again. When he came out, I sighted carefully and pulled the trigger. This time there was no puff of dust indicating a miss, and I raced to the den to claim my prize. But there was no groundhog, and no blood or other sign of a hit. So, assuming I'd missed clean, I began searching the hard packed earth around the den to discover where the bullet had hit. What I found shook me to the roots: a flat lead disc. Apparently I had hit my target, only to have the hollow-point bullet flatten on his tough hide. Now this was a very confounding discovery. To my way of reckoning,

One of the most elegant rimfire rifles ever made was this little-known Steyr-Mannlicher. It was made by the same company that makes the famous Mannlicher center-fire rifles, and the styling is virtually identical. Notice that it has double-set triggers, a shotgun-style trigger guard, folding leaf sight and a beautifully styled, French walnut stock. These guns were imported by Stoeger for a good many years, but for some reason, they never promoted them, and so few were sold. Nonetheless, this is one of the all-time great rimfire hunting rifles. This sample is from my collection.

if a deadly Long-Rifle hollow-point bullet wouldn't kill the groundhog, there was no hope of collecting the five dollar reward.

The problem was so perplexing that I lay awake that night
searching for some solution. One plan that I considered and dis-
missed was sneaking my dad's deer rifle out of the house, and
blasting the groundhog to kingdom come. But if he found out,
it would cost me a yard of hide. Besides, I was fascinated by the
technical mystery of bagging the cagey groundhog with the .22.
And at least as appealing as the cash reward was succeeding
where others, mostly adults, had failed.

My immediate worry was my short supply of Long-Rifle hollow points. After sightin-in the rifle, I was down to only five
or six rounds. After that, I'd have to use solid points.

Solid Points! The thought hit me like a bolt of lightning. The
hollow points collapsed on the tough hide, but the solids would
penetrate.

The next morning I was back in the hedgerow just at day-
break. For a long while I saw nothing, then I spotted a rustle
in the alfalfa. The chuck was out and feeding, but I couldn't see
it. After more minutes of watching the chuck's motion in the
clover, I gave a shrill whistle, and at once the chuck stood up,
looking directly my way. In what seemed the space of a single
heartbeat, the rifle cracked, the chuck went down, and I was
charging after him. He was dead where he had fallen, a bullet
hole at the base of his neck.

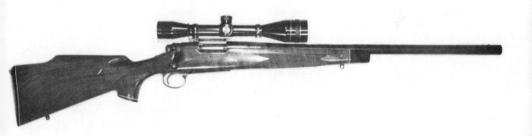

*This rifle is a Remington 40X sporter. It has the same stock as
the Remington Model 700, and the receiver is virtually identical.
This model has the varmint-weight barrel, and is used for
scaled-down silhouette shooting. The scope is a Leupold 10X.
High-quality rimfires such as this bring a lot of grace and style
back to the classic art of rimfire hunting.*

Human nature being what it is, we have the peculiar habit of categorizing .22 caliber rim-fire rifles with barefoot lads in overalls, shooting galleries on carnival midways, and inexpensive semi-guns for plinking vermin and tin cans. This is because nearly every hunter's first shooting experience began with a .22 back when old Rover was a pup. But try looking at it this way: Suppose the .22 rim-fire cartridge were a brand-new development, and just recently announced to the shooting public. Ballistic buffs would wax eloquent about its unique ballistics and accuracy potential, rifle fanciers would dream up all sorts of wonderful—and expensive—rifle configurations adapted to the new round, and all of us would marvel at the round's absolutely perfect suitability for such game as squirrels and a score of var-

This is a Weatherby scope attached to a Model 6¡ Winchester pump-action rimfire. I am an advocate of using scopes on all hunting rifles, especially rimfires. However, I am also very much in favor of mounting a rimfire rifle with the best quality scope one can afford. Preferably a full-sized, big-game scope, which is a better all-around scope for rimfire hunting than is the little so-called rimfire scope. The Weatherby scope shown here is a very excellent "in-between" sight.

Opposite
This squirrel hunter is using an accurate and stylish little rimfire made in Germany by Anschutz and imported by Savage Arms. Anschutz makes one of the best-looking rimfire sporters available today.

Here I do a bit of plinking with one of the all-time great rimfire rifles, the Model 52 Winchester sporter. This model is topped with a 2.5X Redfield scope. The Model 52 sporter is stylishly trim, and as accurate as a target rifle. As a matter of fact, they were an adaptation of Winchester's ultra-accurate Model 52 target model. This gun is no longer produced, and collectors are paying $500 or more for a good sample.

mints and vermin. There is no single center-fire cartridge so ideally suited for any sport that another caliber cannot be substituted with equal success. But this is not true with the .22 rimfire. It is unique.

Also, no other cartridge offers such universal appeal, or comes in nearly so great an array of rifles. There are bolt actions; single shots, tube and clip feeders, pumps, autoloaders, and even side-by-side doubles. Gatling guns have been made in .22 rim-fire, and so have fully-functioning machine guns.

From the standpoint of pure accuracy, probably more money and research time has been spent developing the performance of .22 ammo than any other round. When you buy a box of .22's, their performance is backed by literally millions of dollars worth of development. And the manufacture of .22

ammo is by all odds the most carefully controlled in the shooting industry.

From the accuracy standpoint, the .22 rim-fire can be a remarkable performer. Though volumes are published about the relativity of center-fire accuracy, very little is said about the grouping potential of rim-fire ammo and rifles. Perhaps this is because shooters have no way of controlling the accuracy of .22's, as they do with reloaded center-fire. Or perhaps its just because we assume both ammo and rifles are accurate enough for moderate range shooting.

Actually, just as with center-fires, there is a wide variation in the accuracy of rim-fire rifles *and* ammo. The X-ring of the standard U.S. 100-yard smallbore target is one inch in diameter. A complete smallbore notch at that range consists of forty shots for record, ten shots on each of four targets. At top-flight tournaments, it is not at all uncommon for the better shooters to fire three or four *ten shot* groups, which hit *inside* the one-inch X-ring! When you consider that these groups are fired from the prone position with no artificial support whatever, and often with iron sights, you can get an idea of the accuracy potential of the rim-fire. But needless to say, such tiny groups are fired with super-accurate ammo, such as Winchester's Gold Match, not to mention extremely accurate target rifles.

Just the same, even off-the-shelf grade ammo will usually group inside two inches at 100 yards when fired from a really accurate rifle. But there's the rub, some .22 rifles are not as accurate as they could or should be. Some models are notoriously inaccurate, but, surprisingly, most autoloaders and other repeaters tend to deliver quite good accuracy. It's the cheaper single shots (but not all) that really scatter the shots. This is usually due to poor barrels, weak locking, loose headspace, flimsy receivers, sluggish lock time and bad triggers.

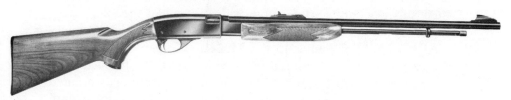

Pump action rimfires have all but disappeared from the modern shooting scene, but Remington still makes its popular Model 572, one of the all-time most successful pump-action rimfires. The one shown here is the BDL deluxe version.

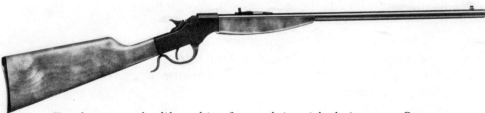

For hunters who like a bit of nostalgia with their sport, Savage has reintroduced the little Stevens Model 74 "Little Favorite." Lots of hunters did their first shooting with this relic from grandfather's time.

These rifles tend to respond better to certain brands of ammo than others, so it's a good idea to try several different brands in order to discover which brand your rifle uses best. In any event, it's almost a certainty that you'll get significantly better accuracy with standard-velocity than with the high-speed ammo. Of particular note in respect to rim-fire ammo is the little known fact that standard velocity .22 ammo is *less* affected by wind than high-speed cartridges. This apparent contradiction of ballistics is due to a phenomenon that occurs at the 1300-1500 feet per second velocity range. At this speed, bullets tend to lose velocity at a higher rate, and are particularly susceptible to the effect of wind.

I usually sight a .22 rim-fire hunting rifle to hit at 50 yards. This is virtually an exact zero for all shots closer than fifty yards. Depending on the ammo used, and how high the sights are above the bore, the point of impact will be six to ten inches low at 100 yards. I also accuracy-test hunting .22's at 50 yards, and expect a good rifle to group inside a nickle when fired from a solid rest.

One of the all-time great .22 hunting rifles was the Winchester Model 52 Sporter. This was built on the same rigid action as their super-accurate M-52 target rifles, and had the same crisp trigger. The barrel was shorter and lighter, and the hand-checkered stocks were similar to the Model 70 Super Grade centerfire. But alas, these beautiful rifles were expensive to make, and the market couldn't bear the cost. Since they were discontinued several years ago, their value has doubled and redoubled until a good specimen, if you're lucky enough to find someone willing to sell, will cost over five hundred dollars. Another little beauty that suffered the same fate was the exquisite Austrian-made Steyr-Mannlicher.

This trim little rifle is the Anschutz Model 184, imported by Savage Arms Company. The Anschutz Company made its reputation with super-accurate rimfire target rifles. Much of this accuracy expertise is incorporated in the rimfire sporter rifles.

Today's class .22's are the Remington Model-700 rim-fire, the Browning take-down autoloader (which comes in three grades), and the top-of-the-line Anschutz sporter. Of these, the Remington is the least seen and the least known. It is a product of the Remington custom shop, and utilizes their 40-X target action noted with a slimmer barrel and a model 700 stock. From all outward appearances, it is a dead-ringer for their Model-700 center-fire rifles. I recently fitted one with a 10X scope, and found the rig to be as accurate as a fine target rifle at 100 yards. The first five shots formed a small cluster. At 50 yards, it is accurate enough to hit a squirrel's eye.

I'm willing to crawl out on a limb and predict that a really finely-built .22 sporter would sell quite well today, regardless of price. There seems to be an undercurrent of buyer trend running toward really good workmanship these days, so there's every reason to believe a really great rim-fire would find a warm response. If it were built right, with a stylish, classic look, an asking price of three hundred dollars wouldn't be out of line.

At present, about the only way to get a really great .22 rim-fire hunting rifle, other than buying a used Steyr, M-52 or M-700, is to have one built by a top-notch custom riflesmith. The first step is to buy a used Winchester Model-52, or Remington-37 target rifle, then have its barrel turned down and shortened to sporter dimensions. Then have a fine sporter-style stock fitted, along with such niceties as long softees, restyled trigger guard, etc. The total project, if done by a top craftsman, may cost upwards of a thousand dollars, but the beauty of it is that the rifle will never be worth less than what you paid for it. Perhaps this sounds a bit rich for a lowly twenty-two, but to my way of thinking, squirrel hunting is one of the really elegant sports, ranking with grouse shooting in Scotland, or snipe shooting in

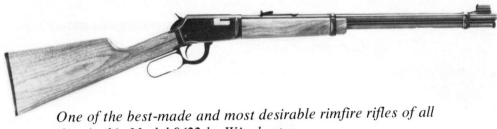

One of the best-made and most desirable rimfire rifles of all time is this Model 9422 by Winchester.

Kashmir, and deserves a truly elegant firearm. But for the more prosaic—and practical—the selection of .22 hunting rifles on to-day's market is vast—far too many to describe here.

The things to look for in a suitable hunting .22, once you've decided how much you want to spend, are pretty much the same things you look for in a big-game rifle. A crisp-breaking trigger pull is a tremendous aid to good shooting, and light weight is de-sirable only up to a point. If you select an autoloader or pump, you'll be wise to choose a model that can be field stripped, or at least has a good-sized ejection port for easy cleaning. The most common cause of functional failure among self-feeders is an accumulation of grimes in the mechanism.

The sights that come on most rim-fires are only mediocre at best, but this is no problem because a scope, or peep sight, will probably be used anyway. Most of today's rim-fire models come with receivers already grooved for easy mounting of clamp-type scope mounts. And quite a few of the little inexpen-sive .22 type scopes come complete with this type of mounting system.

However, for really top performance from a rim-fire hunt-ing rifle, I strongly recommend a full size (one-inch tube) scope of the type you'd use on a center-fire big game rifle. First of all, with their longer eye relief and wider field of view, these longer scopes are a lot easier to use. And second, the finer optics and relative brightness make your aim a lot more precise. This is especially apparent when you can only see half a squirrel's head peeking at you over a hickory limb. I usually use either a 4X or 6X scope, but a variable power model in the 2.5-7X range would be perfect for just about every situation. This, of course, is not to say that the little .22 style scopes aren't satisfactory. They are. When I was a teen-ager, I used a Model B-6 Weaver that then sold for about ten dollars. I thought it was the greatest thing since summer vacation, and shot enough crows, squirrels, rats

A stylish-looking rimfire autoloader with a big-gun look is Winchester's Model 490 autoloader. Note the sleek lines and big-gun styling.

and rabbits with it to fill a barge. But when I graduated to a full-size scope, the improvement was immediately noticeable. Of course these full-size scopes mean you'll have to spend even more money on a special set of rings. Most scope and mount makers manufacture one-inch rings that clamp directly onto grooved .22 receivers. The best rule when selecting the scope is the same as selecting the rifle—get the best you can afford. Weaver, Leupold, Redfield and Bushnell are excellent choices.

Remember, a .22 rim-fire caliber hunting rifle is a *hunting rifle*, and not just another .22.

Woodchuck Hunting

Bert Popowski

Call him what you wish, the lowly groundhog has had a wider impact on the rifle hunting of varmint or pest targets than any other North American creature. In the east, he is known as the woodchuck or marmot, sometimes the pasture pig. In the highlands of the west, he goes by the name of whistler, because of his piercing shrill when alarmed—or rock-chuck, because he often dwells in the crevices between shattered mountain rocks. Like the crow, which has long been the favorite of shotgunners, the woodchuck is the favorite target of innumerable riflemen.

The woodchuck has provided so much exacting sport that several rifle calibers were designed specifically or converted for this purpose. The rifle needed a gentle report and easy recoil, and a small bullet of adequate velocity to disintegrate readily, yet powerful enough to kill surely and cleanly. It was only after decades of woodchuck hunting that attention was paid to shooting woodchucks, and other targets, with a minimum of carcass damage.

The first of these was the .22 Hornet, a modernization of the black-powder .22 Winchester Center Fire dating back to the late 1800's. The original Hornets were custom-made, and this cartridge was actually factory-produced by Winchester around 1930, before any manufacturer made rifles to shoot it. Savage made the first bolt-action Hornet rifles about 1932, and Winchester produced its famous Model 54 Hornet a year or so later. Hornet-chambered rifles have been available ever since.

Wherever it lives, the woodchuck is like a power mower, and keeps its portly belly comfortably stuffed with the tastiest greenery surrounding its chosen den sites. It doesn't need springs or waterholes, but gets its liquids from the dew on its food, occasional rains or the moisture in the succulent plants it prefers. By doing a judicious amount of traveling, it manages to find ample assorted foods for a balanced diet. As a general rule, its den is dug past a narrow entrance where enemies can't dig him out, and has a hidden exit for emergency escape. But the path where it wanders for food is also marked by sundry transient "motel" burrows into which it can dodge if it encounters a hostile coyote, fox, dog or other meat-eating foe. Eagles and the larger hawks and owls aren't averse to a meal of tender young chuck.

All this digging doesn't endear him to landowners. They object to gluttonous raids on succulent alfalfas and clovers, as well as small grain and grass crops. Woodchucks that invade truck gardens can become enormously destructive; and stock owners especially fear the leg-breaking hazards provided by numerous chuck burrows.

So visiting riflemen searching for targets find ready welcomes in wide-open woodchuck country where land holdings are of substantial size. In such spacious areas, the louder reports of deer-hunting calibers can serve to keep hunters sharp of accuracy and nerve between seasons, and bring no objections from harried landowners beset by woodchuck abundance; unless those landowners are themselves chuck hunters and want to keep the current crop handy for their own recreational varmint shooting.

Within the last half-dozen years, the rising prices of such fur-bearers as fox, coyote and bobcat have spawned a mixed breed of riflemen. Some of them are strictly deer hunters, others hunt varmints by preference, but all of them are willing to take a pop at any handy fur-bearers they encounter. Hunters going specifically after furs operate only during the cold months when furs are prime and in solid demand. What makes them different from the strictly varmint hunters, including those after woodchucks, is their desire to kill cleanly, and to pick up their game with only lightly-damaged pelts. When the value of a fine red fox or coyote pelt, for instance, depreciates from a potential $70 to a mere $30, just because it is badly bullet-ripped, that hurts the fur hunter in his billfold. And when a bullet-torn bobcat hide plummets from a potential top of $200 down to $75 or less, that hurts even worse. So varmint hunters can now operate on a year-round basis, polishing their marksmanship on woodchucks and crows during the summer to be ready for when cold weather brings on deer season and makes furs prime.

*The author with a mountain woodchuck taken in the Gold
Coast area.*

In order to avoid a big share of both meat damage on edible
game and pelt damage on furbearer hides, they use reduced
loads. Exhaustive experimental shooting has proved that almost
every rifle and handgun can be used with moderate loads to produce fur pelts that bring top dollar. Most varmints are nonsal-
vageable, and the hunters therefore prefer high-velocity loads
that tear them apart and kill instantly. But when used on such
choice game as turkey or deer, such fast loads should be tamed
considerably to avoid producing extensive blood-clotting.

It has been proved that both high velocity and bullet construction are jointly responsible for excessive meat and pelt
damage. Woodchuck pelts are virtually worthless, but the meat
of young chucks is fine eating, certainly just as tasty as that of
raccoon and opossum if properly cooked.

Experimenting hand loaders have learned that bullet velocities ranging from 1500 to 2000 feet per second (fps) at the rifle
muzzle are best for taking small game neatly—from squirrels and
rabbits to game birds like turkeys. These are also good velocities

The .22 semiautomatic Weatherby XXII loaded with CCI .22 Stinger hollow-points does good work at moderate ranges.

for woodchucks that are to be skinned, gutted and prepared for cooking.

The furbearers mentioned above have much vitality—and looser, elastic hides—and can stand velocities ranging from 2300 to 2600 FPS before their pelts show undesirable and costly damage. This is all right for varmint shooting of species that are to be discarded, but if used on such choice game as turkeys, or woodchucks intended for eating, much meat is damaged.

Jerry Popowski, with one young and one adult woodchuck bagged, glasses for another target with his Remington .222.

The hunter who goes to 2800 to 3000 fps—a thrifty velocity range for deer—will find that his furbearing pelts will show considerable damage at this level. And anything of higher fps velocity than that will "bullet splash" a lot of meat, so much that it has to be cut away and discarded because of messy blood clotting. If his bullet strikes on choice eating meat, a hunter may thus retrieve only a fraction of the excellent venison he might otherwise enjoy from a prime meat animal. And what happens to deer will occur even more dramatically on any of the smaller animals.

The woodchuck hunter thus can go two ways, according to his personal inclination. If he enjoys hearing his bullets whang violently into his targets, he can use the highest velocity of which his rifle is capable. In some cases, such high-velocity loads will actually explode varmint game at the point of impact and all along the bullet's course. Such hits leave no doubt of the fatalities they inflict, since the victims are generally a shambles when hit.

Or, if the hunter wants to study the effects of milder loads, he can use the reduced loads I've mentioned for the fur-bearing species. If he is a painstaking shot who takes pride in precision placement of his hits on vitals, he may even want to go to bullet velocities suitable for birds and small game, as woodchucks aren't really hard to kill. I've taken many of them with ordinary rimfire .22's, both in rifles and handguns, and the Winchester .22 rimfire magnum is deadly on chucks, though I'll freely admit that it's much more sport to take them at long range with precision-tuned center-fire rifles. Like all wildlife, even when abun-

An accurate .22 scope-sighted rifle, loaded with Long Rifle, hollow-point ammunition, is a deadly combination for woodchucks in up to 100-yard ranges.

A spot overlooking a rocky hillside frequently provides an excellent location from which to spot and shoot woodchucks.

dant enough to become nuisances to crops and cattle, they're still entitled to sure but considerate reduction.

Woodchucks are interesting creatures with some unusual habits that merit close evaluation, but some of the myths concerning them should be considered skeptically. (Like their fabled annual emergence on February 2 for Groundhog Day, when they're supposed to forecast how much longer winter will last. If they see their shadows on that sunny date, winter is expected to continue for six more weeks. But if the day is overcast, says this myth, spring will come earlier.)

During a prolonged warm spell in the Deep South, a snoozing chuck might be tempted to awaken and emerge for a very brief yawn and stretch—and a weather forecast. But in most woodchuck ranges, the probability of such a break in his winterlong snooze is remote. In fact, woodchucks are such solid hibernators that, if the spring weather turns cold and inclement after they do emerge, it is no unusual thing for them to retire for several days, even weeks, of further extended slumber. They prefer to emerge to lush greenery when their vegetarian buffet has become more generous.

There are cases of woodchucks emerging from hibernation during the winter, sometimes in quite bitter weather. Those very rare specimens are doomed to death in one of several ways. First, illness or disability caused them to put on less than the

Here's a grandpappy woodchuck, shot at nearly 300 yards by Jerry Popowski with his .222 Remington rifle, fitted with a Bushnell six-power telescopic sight.

sustaining conditioning of winter tallow needed to keep them warmly insulated during their long sleep. Consequently, they awaken due to cold and hunger, and emerge in an unseasonal attempt to feed. Second, some chucks are forced to hibernate in unsuitable quarters. They are then seeking shelter from the cold which will probably kill them anyway during that search. And finally, some are parasitized to such a high degree that the biting and blood-sucking of body pests causes restlessness they simply can't sleep through.

In all such cases, the result is freezing to death, instead of merely "sleeping their lives away," as is the case with superannuated animals. A woodchuck in robust health generally uses the summer months to prepare for winter, both by putting on a heavy, nourishing and heat-insulating blanket of tallow, and by digging a burrow well below the frostline, and insulating it with a comfortable wall-to-wall blanket of grasses.

I have personally encountered only one winter-emerging chuck, and I repeatedly sighted him during sunny but icy-cold weather. I finally shot him for examination to account for his unorthodox behavior. He was nearly bald, and his skin was covered with scabs from thousands of flea bites. He was thin in flesh, and had evidently been tormented so much that he hadn't been able to sustain healthy hibernating sleep. Even if he had been able to rid himself of his unwelcome guests and had found a warm den for the balance of the winter, it is highly improbable that he could have survived until the next green grass arrived. So my bullet, originally fired to satisfy my curiosity, actually put him out of hopeless misery.

Even in normally healthy condition, woodchucks exhibit some odd traits. They emerge when spring's first green grasses arrive, and their days are spent alternately feeding greedily and freshening up last year's burrows for their summer homes. They instinctively know that such succulent food will deteriorate during the hot summer, so they'll need an extension of their feeding range. But when they've laid on a thick and almost disabling blanket of tallow by late summer and early autumn, they suddenly become astonishingly scarce. A thriving chuck settlement suddenly becomes a virtual ghost town.

This vanishing act is largely due to their intolerance of hot weather after they've laid on a suitable blanket of tallow. During these hot days, they even give up their betwixt-snack habit of climbing atop handy stumps or rocks for lazy siestas. Instead, they ignore the dry and tasteless vegetation of that season, and

There's no healthier recreation for a pair of buddies than going woodchucking on a warm summer day.

retire to cool burrows for prolonged snoozes. This is what biologists call estivation, and is actually a prolonged underground siesta. Presumably, during this semi-dormant stage, woodchucks try out their hibernating dens for size for the full hibernation to come later. It is possible that they also build their winter nests during this semi-dormant period, for when they vanish from sight, there are usually some spilled tufts of dry grasses in and about the mouths of the dens that seem to be most conveniently situated and have been most heavily used during the busy days of summer. Instinctively, they know to emerge next spring in an area of abundant food and comparatively easy detection of enemies while they're still quite groggy.

While their transient escape dens may be shallow and makeshift, the hibernating dens are dug deep enough to be below frostline. They also avoid marshes, and are above the level of sub-surface water that might flood their hibernating dens. They

Woodchucks are large enough to furnish targets for fine long-range marksmanship. This pair of half-grown young were taken at 200 yards by Jerry Popowski, using a .222 Remington, wearing a Bushnell six-power scope sight.

are thus cool during the summer, and the sleeping chamber, when fitted with a loose plug of grass, retains enough body heat to comfortably sustain hibernation.

Some eastern states have humane wildlife laws that prohibit the shooting of adult woodchucks during the spring-summer period when they bear their young. This prevents orphaning the nursing young until they've made the transition from milk to succulent grasses. If captured at such times, young chucks make entertaining pets, though they may be damaging to vegetable and flower gardens if allowed to range in them. Usually such seasons remain closed until haying is completed, when the shortened grasses make for higher visibility, thus enabling observation of the development of the young, and revealing suitable targets for riflemen.

Shooting at partially-concealed game with today's high-velocity calibers often results in the deflection or disintegration of bullets. But a metal whistle of high pitch is often very handy to make woodchucks show themselves in fairly thick and high cover. They then stand upright and, once the hunter has roughly located them, he can get set, sound his whistle again, and get good clean shots when his alerted game surveys its surroundings for danger.

Since woodchucks alert each other to danger from one end of a wide valley to the other, the successful hunter makes cautious approaches. Rock-chucks pass the word to each other along mountainous ridges. The typical wounded-rabbit varmint call should never be used on them. Chucks recognize it as the desperate scream of terror of a rabbit. Since rabbit foes also occasionally dine on woodchucks, what is feared by one is hazardous to the other. A shrieking varmint call thus is all it takes to send them diving underground.

There are several basic ways of hunting woodchucks. The simplest is simply to scan good chuck country with binoculars, find a few targets, and go to work with rifle and accuracy-proven hand loads. Another method is to work boldly into the middle of known woodchuck habitat, then partially conceal oneself and whistle them into sight by copying their own characteristic danger signals to set them in motion. Hidden chucks close to their burrows will often stand upright and reveal themselves for shots. And those that have wandered some distance from quick shelter will usually gallop clumsily denward before they assume their vertical reconnaissance stance. The hunter can then choose shots at his favorite ranges, moving to a new location only when he has exhausted the in-range area of suitable targets.

The patient hunter is occasionally treated to the sight of other animal hunters seeking woodchuck dinners. I once saw a golden eagle zip down on a rock-chuck sunning atop a large slab of rock. The chuck's den was probably beneath that granitic slab, but he never made it. The eagle clenched its deadly talons into the chuck's vitals, and swept it off onto the open sod with the velocity of its attack. The kill was made so neatly and rap-

In many eastern states, the woodchuck is legally protected until haying is done. But then the chuck is exposed to the stalking rifleman.

idly, and with such furious speed, that it seemed a violently hazardous neighborhood for careless rock-chucks for miles around. Presumably, large owls and hawks also take their toll of such handy fare, especially bagging the young and careless chucks that stray away from their homes.

Foxes, coyotes and bobcats dine on chucks whenever they can surprise and overpower them. Pairs of these predators have been reported using a hunting plan that is cleverly efficient. One of them will stroll openly past an exposed woodchuck, making no attempt at concealment or any menacing moves. Naturally, the chuck dives underground. But his curiosity brings him to the surface to watch this enemy stroll calmly on its way, getting farther away by the minute. Meanwhile, the second of that hunting pair has slipped stealthily within a jump of the den. When the watching chuck emerges and rivets its attention on the visible departing killer, the concealed killer pounces on a fat and tasty dinner.

Woodchucks love to find sunny spots on which to take the air, and from which they can spot any oncoming intruder.

An adult woodchuck is a mean fighter, as many a brash farm dog has learned. When cornered, it "chitters" its teeth threateningly. And when attacked, its beaver-like rodent teeth go deep and meet in a punishing hold. Any dog that is nailed on its face is only too happy to call off the attack, if only the woodchuck will also call it quits. Foxes and coyotes avoid such wounding by seizing their prey at the small of the back, and then shaking them so vigorously that the back is broken. With their hind legs immobilized, such crippled chucks can only drag themselves with the forepaws, and are readily finished off. The badger, a mighty fang-to-fang fighter in its own right, and with formidable claws to back up its dentures, is the only natural enemy that doesn't avoid such confrontations. If he fancies a handy woodchuck den for his own use, he preempts it and, if the homesteading inhabitant objects, he both kills and eats him.

One of the finest chuck-hunting spots I have ever known was an area we came to call the Gold Coast. In its day, it had yielded a good amount of placer gold, and a handful of old-time prospectors still lived there and mined the tributaries of Ruby Creek. Among them was "Woodchuck Bob" Carter, a gentle and nature-loving soul who supported himself by panning gold in the summers, and then went on winter relief.

We had a standing order from him for any young wood-chucks we shot in that verdant valley. "Iffen yuh kill enny young 'uns I'd be proud to have 'em," was his regular request. Since he batched and did his own cooking, I suppose young woodchucks furnished a good share of his daily protein. At any rate, we provided what we could. In exchange, he showed us how to pan gold and, on one "clean-up day," we watched him wash out over $50 worth of fine gold before sending it in to the Denver mint. The yellow metal didn't sell at today's inflated prices, but nonetheless, the money it brought met many of Carter's daily needs.

Woodchucks can provide the means of teaching pinpoint marksmanship to the tyro rifleman, and to give him confidence when going after more serious game when deer and turkey seasons open. Chucks are amply wary to require crafty stalking, and have sufficient life tenacity to require precise placement of bullets. After being hunted a little, they provide worthy foes for priming even the most exacting big-game hunters. The western and northern guides I've talked to are in complete accord on one point: Eastern woodchuck hunters are their preferred game-hunting clients. After a hunter has learned his lessons of estimating range and its trajectory, as well as wind and its drift, he knows how to efficiently apply those lessons to his next season. For the more field experience acquired, the better the hunter knows his game and its habits, and the more rewarding are his sundry stalks for it.

It is an established truism that you can't shoot any better than you can see. Translated into productive woodchucking, that means that binoculars are a great aid in spotting semi-concealed targets, and telescopic sights are a vast aid in making pinpoint hits. For when the first green grass stretches out to a concealable height, the earlier easy-to-see targets have vanished. That's just as well, since chucks are then raising their young, and no sensible rifleman will then kill adults, orphan the young and rapidly reduce his sport. It's best to wait until after the first cutting of hay, when the young are nearing the all-grass-diet stage of development. Those spring weeks while the young are being raised to weaning age can be used for spotting dens. It's as much

Two boys, outfitted with a Winchester .22 rifle, wearing a four-power Weaver scope, can have a lot of sport reducing overabundant ground squirrels.

sport as the actual shooting, and yields many insights into behavior patterns.

There are three considerations for efficient glassware for woodchuck hunting: power, weight and size. A large powerful binocular may be fine to carry in your vehicle and view from there. But, when you intend to hang them from your neck during actual stalking, their weight and size are an important factor. So binoculars are best in the 6×30 to 7×35 range, preferably built on light-weight aluminum-alloy type frames. Then shorten the neck-strap so that you can slip them on or off past your ears. They will then ride high on your chest and not bounce on your belly when walking or jogging into good shooting position.

Similarly, the rifle's scope needn't be one of the long target types, over half of the length of the gun's barrel. Nor should it be of such high magnification that the outfit looks as if you've hitched a spotting scope atop your shooting-iron. Unless you want to specialize on shots at the extreme edge of your rifle's

Woodchucks are among the best known all-winter hibernators.

potential range, there's no reason for it to run past six-power magnification. In variable scopes, the 2×7-power is about right for woodchucks, and even then, you'll seldom set it to maximum magnification. In variable scopes, the 2×7 power is about right shoot all that much better. It then also magnifies rifle joggle from heart-beat, nerve and muscle shakiness. It also seems to melt the sighting reticles into wavy lines when mirage is prevalent. But if low-power scopes are employed, such joggling and mirage smudging are minimized. All this adds up to clearer and steadier sight pictures, leading to accurate bullet placement.

Depending on his local surroundings and what he has to work with, the woodchuck hunter can use most of the rifles suitable for American game for woodchucks, especially if he hand loads to the modest velocities heretofore recommended. But if he prefers to literally shatter his chuck targets, he can accomplish that with full-power commercial ammunition and maximum hand loads. I don't recommend that, for such high velocities automatically invite rapid bore erosion and shorter barrel life. Also, such top-velocity loads are seldom as accurate as those of more moderate pressures.

The smallest calibers aren't necessarily the least destructive. For instance, the tiny .17 caliber has to be loaded to velocities between 3500 and nearly 4000 fps to stabilize its 25-grain bullet. But such velocity, matched only by the .220 Swift and the older .22-250, also invites enormous air friction, which rapidly slows such bullets in flight. It also tends to increase wind drift if any significant breeze is moving. All in all, the serious woodchucker in populated communities is well advised to stay with the historic .22 Hornet with its mild report, or the .222 with reduced loads, which produce similar minimum noise.

When using any of the popular deer calibers, whether with regular or reduced loads, the rifleman needs large acreages to avoid becoming a nuisance. Even then he had better have the full approval of landowners on whose acres he hunts. This includes a strict adherence to staying out of pastures containing livestock and far away from farm or ranch buildings. An unexpected or inappropriate rifle blast will often end an otherwise cordial woodchuck hunt.

In the spacious areas in which I hunt woodchucks, I like a super-accurate and heavy-barreled Winchester Model 54 in .250 caliber. I use 100-grain bullets in it, ahead of 36 grains of 4064 powder, since that rifle's 12-inch twist has proven able to handle them with superb accuracy. Up to 300 yards, it is a very fortunate chuck that survives beyond a shot or two.

Competitive
Rifle
Shooting

Part III

Competition Shooting

Gary L. Anderson

Why do people participate in sports? The skier is likely seeking the thrill of speed and precariousness which his rush down the mountain gives him. The long-distance runner is trying to see how far he can push the limits of his body's endurance. The weight lifter is after the development of ultimate strength. The golfer returns to the course week after week because he finds satisfaction in developing and demonstrating a demanding and very specific skill.

Thrill, speed, strength, endurance, skill—all of these are elements of the experience. They are the reasons people keep coming back to their particular sport. Virtually every sport is unique because of the way it emphasizes one of these elements of the sports experience.

In this context, shooting is unmistakably a skill sport. The heart and soul of shooting is hitting the target, or better yet, the center of the target. Learning, developing and demonstrating the skill of consistently hitting a difficult target is what shooting is all about.

The most important thing about a sports skill is that it must be compared to a standard, it must be measurable. In golf, skill is measured by the number of strokes taken; in bowling, by the number of pins knocked down; and in shooting, by scores fired on a target.

There are targets for many different kinds of rifles and distances, but almost all of them have scoring rings with values ranging from ten points on down. One new shooting game, metal silhouette, uses a hit and miss system on game-shaped steel targets, instead of the traditional paper target. In either case, the objective is to get the highest score possible.

Many people who have not been involved in competitive shooting don't realize that target shooting is a sport just as golf, skiing, tennis, gymnastics and archery are sports. Shooting is, in fact, one of the most popular of all sports. It now ranks as the fifth most popular participation sport in the entire world. Only two other sports, track and boxing, regularly attract more participating nations in the Olympics.

The names of shooting champions like Lanny Bassham, Margaret Murdock, Lones Wigger and Jack Writer are not often household words in this country, but on the streets of Switzerland, Germany or many East European countries, they would be recognized much quicker than American baseball and football heroes.

One of the myths that people outside of shooting commonly hold is that it is dangerous. The truth is that shooting is one of the safest of all sports. Accidents in target shooting, in contrast to many sports, are virtually unheard of. The reason for this outstanding safety record is that very strict safety procedures are practiced on all shooting ranges. The only time a bolt or other action is ever closed on a range is when the shooter is on the firing line and is actually ready to shoot.

Shooting is a life-time sport open to both men and women. It exhibits some of the widest age variations found in any sport. Organized shooting programs begin for youngsters as young as eight shooting BB guns in the Jaycee Shooting Education program. Smallbore prone competitors have been known to stay active into their seventies.

It is now an accepted fact that women can compete equally with men in rifle-shooting events. Five of the ten best scores ever fired in the world in the 50-meter standard rifle event have been fired by women. Margaret Murdock, an American shooter, not only holds the open world record for the standing position with the smallbore rifle, but she also won a silver medal in the last Olympic Games at Montreal in open competition, with a score numerically identical to that of the gold medal winner. In what has become a common occurence, three of the ten members of the 1977 College All-American Rifle Team were women.

Overleaf: *United States shooting teams regularly participate in Olympic World Shooting Championships, Pan American Games and other international competitions. Since 1964, American rifle shooters have won more medals than shooters from any other country.*

The real essence of shooting is not strength or speed or endurance, but rather the learning of a very special skill that must then be demonstrated under the pressure of competition. In most sports, nervousness from competition can be used to make the athlete jump higher, run faster or hit harder. The shooter, in comparison, must learn the self-control and mental discipline necessary to suppress these natural human reactions. This makes shooting, in many respects, a sport of the mind, rather than a sport of the muscles and body.

The skill levels attained by champion shooters may seem unbelievable when compared to what are often considered feats of marksmanship. A deer hunter who can hit the small shoulder area of a deer at 200 yards in the standing position is considered an excellent shot, but a good 300 meter rifle shooter will routinely place all forty of his offhand competition shots inside a 12 inch circle at 300 meters (330 yards) with 90 percent of those shots striking inside the 8-inch 9 ring.

A varmint hunter is considered excellent if he can make hits at 300 or 400 yards with a scope-sighted rifle, but the high-power rifle shooter is disappointed if even one of his twenty shots at 600 yards falls outside of the 12-inch ten ring, and he does all his shooting with iron sights. Any hunter who can regularly hit running targets is considered good, but the international running boar shooter must routinely hit a moving target, which has a ten ring the size of a 50-cent piece, at 50 meters.

Competitive Rifle Events

The skill levels of good competitive shooters may seem amazing to people who have never tried target shooting, but the important thing is that shooting is a sport where natural ability is far less important than the effort that is made to become a good shooter. The first step in responding to this challenge is to choose a shooting event in which to get involved.

Competitive rifle events are usually divided into international and national competitions. International competitions are the events that make up the Olympic, World Championship and Pan American Games shooting programs. The rules for these events are made up by the International Shooting Union (UIT), the governing body of world shooting.

The more difficult targets and courses of fire, and the special challenge of world-level competition, make international events the specialty of our very best shooter-athletes. The stories of six-and eight-hour training days put in by young swimmers and figure skaters can also be told about young shooters. Only the all-out dedication and training of a world-class athlete will permit a shooter to reach championship levels in those events.

International shooting events obviously enjoy their highest popularity with the very best shooters who are willing to engage in the serious training programs they require. In spite of their difficulty, they are rapidly becoming more popular, especially among young shooters. All college shooting is now done according to international rules. Junior shooting is becoming increasingly international, while even air-rifle shooting in the United States is now done exclusively with international rules. A brief description of the international rifle events follows:

300-Meter Free Rifle. This is the oldest and most prestigious of the international rifle events. It was on the program of the second Olympics in 1900, and has been in every world championship since the first one in 1897. Center-fire rifles not larger than 8mm are fired at a 300-meter target with a 10-centimeter (3.9 inch) ten ring. The two most popular cartridges for this event are the .308 Winchester and the 7.62mm Russian. The standard course of fire is 40 shots in the prone position, 40 shots standing and 40 shots kneeling. The rifle may weigh as much as 17.6 pounds, and special accessories like hook buttplates, set triggers, thumbhole stocks and palm rests are common.

50-Meter Three Position. This event began as a way to practice 300-meter shooting, and has gradually become more popular than its parent because of range and cost limitations of big-bore shooting. The rifle appears the same as the free rifle, except that it is a .22 rim-fire. The 50-meter target has a .48-inch ten ring, and is an exact reduction of the 300-meter target. The same 120-shot, three-position course of fire is also used.

300-Meter Standard Rifle. This was once an army or military rifle event, but it has become an event that is simply restricted to center-fire rifles with standard stocks and without special accessories like palm rests. hook buttplates and set triggers. The rifles for this 60-shot, three-position event cannot weigh over 5 kilograms (11 lbs.).

50-Meter Standard Rifle. The same equipment limitations that are used for 300-meter standard rifle also apply in this 60-shot, three-position event that is fired with a .22 rim-fire rifle. Beginning in 1977, 50-meter standard rifle competition will be restricted to women and juniors.

50-Meter Prone. This event attracts more individual entries than any other event in the Olympics. The equipment rules are the same as for the smallbore, three-position rifle. Since the prone position requires a lot less training than kneeling and standing, some shooters who don't have the time necessary for three-position shooting have specialized in this match.

Air Rifle. This is both the newest and the fastest-growing shooting event. In West Germany alone, there are nearly a million active air-rifle competitors. Air rifles are identical to standard rifles in weight and balance. At the 10-meter air-gun distance, half-minute of angle accuracy capabilities are common with these .177 caliber rifles. Only the standing position is used in this event.

National competition events are even more diverse than international events, and are often looked upon as recreational sports. They fall in the same category as the weekend skiing trip, the evening bowling league or the weekly golf game. They utilize easier targets and require less practice time than international events. Many of them trace their ancestry to American military rifle competitions. National recreational competitive rifle events include:

Smallbore Gallery. This is the most popular event in America. It is used in winter indoor rifle leagues throughout the country and involves either three- or four-position shooting on indoor 50-foot ranges with a rim-fire rifle. The rifles used may be international position rifles or standard rifles. In some areas of the country, all gallery shooting is done with target telescopes of 15 or 20 power.

Smallbore Prone. This is primarily an accuracy and wind doping event shot outdoors at 50 yards, 50 meters and 100 yards. A typical match has four 40-shot matches with iron sights on one day and four 40-shot matches with a telescope the next day. Since prone position shooting skill is easier to acquire and retain and demands less training, outdoor prone competition is an ideal event for a shooter who doesn't want to spend a lot of time practicing between matches.

High-Power Match Rifle. This event may be the best all-around test of a shooter's ability. This competition combines slow-fire shooting at 200 yards standing and at 600 yards prone,

Lanny Bassham, Olympic smallbore rifle champion in 1976 and World 300-meter rifle champion in 1974, in the kneeling position. The rifle is a .22 rim-fire three-position rifle.

Two-time Olympic gold medalist, Lones Wigger, looks through his spotting scope to check his last shot. He is shooting a small bore rifle in prone position.

with rapid-fire shooting at 200 and 300 yards in sitting and prone positions. Slow-fire, rapid-fire, position shooting, short-range, long-range, wind doping, knowledge of a rifle's zero and an unparalleled test of rifle accuracy and reliability—all these are part of the high-power match rifle game. Any center-fire rifle may be used, but the .308 Winchester is the overwhelming favorite because of its combination of inherent accuracy, long-range wind-bucking ability and the availability of excellent .30-caliber match bullets. Bolt-action repeaters are needed for rapid fire, while standard-type stocks are normally used. Almost all the ammunition fired in this game is hand loaded by the shooter himself. A special version of high-power rifle shooting involves firing at 1000 yards in the prone position.

Military Rifle. The course of fire in this event is identical to that used for high-power match rifle shooting. Both military and match rifles often compete alongside each other in the same match. M-14 or M-1 service rifles especially made accurate for competition are used. One of the most sought-after awards in shooting, the Distinguished Rifleman's Badge, awarded by the National Board for the Promotion of Rifle Practice, can be won only in special service rifle matches.

Metal Silhouette. This fast-growing high-power rifle event started in Mexico, and has been rapidly spreading from the southwest United States into the rest of the country. In this event, metal silhouettes shaped like chickens, turkeys, javelinas and sheep are fired on at distances of 200, 300, 385 and 500 meters. All shooting is done offhand with the sporter-type rifles that cannot weigh over 10 lbs., 2 oz. with a telescope attached. Six to ten power scopes are preferred.

Equipment

Successful target shooting requires the right equipment, and for many shooters, acquiring and working with new items of target equipment provides a special enjoyment of its own. There are certain basic items of equipment that are necessary even for the beginner, and many other items that can be added as experience and interest increases. An adequate set of target equipment includes:

Rifle. There are as many different target rifles as there are target-rifle events. The table printed here indicates rifle features that are needed or recommended for these events.

Ammunition. Shooting winning scores in most competitive rifle events requires a rifle/ammunition combination that will produce minute of angle or better groups. The selection of proper ammunition is essential to achieving this level of accuracy. Rim-fire riflemen use standard-velocity ammunition for training, or if they are new shooters, special match-grade ammunition should be used for serious competition.

There are wide variations in quality from one lot of ammunition to the next. A lot that will not group well in tests with one rifle may be outstanding in another rifle. The only way to find out which ammunition to use is to get samples from a number of different lots, and to test them on a bench rest, or from a supported prone position.

Except for service-rifle shooters who have access to 7.62mm or .30-06 National Match ammunition, all ammunition for high-power match rifles must be hand loaded. The process of loading match ammunition is similar to any other kind of hand loading. Match-grade bullets and components are used to hand load target-quality ammunition.

Rear Sight. Most shooting events are restricted to the metallic or "peep" sights, although some do permit the use of a telescope. In either case, the sights should be specifically designed for target shooting, and should have windage and elevation knobs that will precisely move the strike of the bullet a distance equal to $\frac{1}{4}$ or $\frac{1}{6}$ inch at 100 yards for each click of adjustment.

The author, Gary Anderson, with the 300-meter free rifle he used to win gold medals in the 1964 and 1968 Olympics.

EVENT	CALIBER	ACTION	WEIGHT	STOCK	SPECIAL FEATURES
300m Free Rifle	.308 Winc .30-06	Bolt action, single shot, solid bottom	15-17 lbs.	Thumbhole stock, hook buttplate, palm rest & rail	4-8 ounce, two-stage trigger recommended
50m Three Position		Bolt action, single shot	15-17 lbs.	Same as above	Same as above
300m Standard Rifle	.308 Winc	Bolt action, with 5 shot magazine	11 lbs.	Standard stock	1.5 Kg (3.2 lbs.) trigger required
50m Standard Rifle	.22 l.r.	Bolt action, single shot	11 lbs.	Standard stock	
50m Prone	.22 l.r.	Bolt action, single shot	12-14 lbs.	Special prone stock with standard pistol grip	Single-stage trigger preferred
Air Rifle	.177	Pneumatic, single-stroke cocking	11 lbs.	Standard stock	
50 ft. Gallery	.22 l.r.	Bolt action, single shot	15-17 with free rifle; 11-13 with standard stock	Thumbhole with accessories or standard stock	15 to 20 power telescope recommended
Smallbore Prone	.22 l.r.	Bolt action, single shot	12-14 lbs.	Standard or special prone stock	Both metallic and scope sights required
High-Power Rifle	.308 .30-06	Bolt action, with 5-shot magazine	12-14 lbs.	Standard stock	1-10 or 1-12 twist barrels needed for heavy bullets
Military Rifle	7.62 NATO .30-06	M-1 or M-14 Service rifle	9 lbs.	Issue Stock	Glass bedding and accurization
Metal Silhouette	.308 7mm/308	Bolt action, with 5 shot magazine	10 lbs. with scope	Sporter stock	6-10 power telescope recommended

Front Sight. The key feature of a target front sight is the aiming element used to align the rifle with the bull. It can be either a square-topped post or an aperture or ring that fits inside a front-sight hood. The hooded front sight is standard on most target rifles, and is designed to permit the interchanging of front-sight inserts.

Sling. A sling is always used in prone, kneeling and sitting positions, but it is not permitted in standing. The most common target slings are 1½-inch wide straps of leather with buckles that permit adjustments for length.

Ear protectors. Ear protection is necessary in all shooting events except air-rifle shooting. The best protection is provided by ear muffs, and either ear muffs or ear plugs should be worn anytime shooting is being done.

Shooting Jacket. The purpose of the jacket is to protect the shoulders and elbows, and to pad the arm from sling pressure. A beginning shooter can improvise a jacket from a light-weight leather or cloth jacket, while an advanced shooter will want to purchase a jacket especially made for target shooting that has pads sewn on the arms and right shoulder.

Glove or Mitt. A glove or mitten is used to protect the hand from rifle and sling pressure. Commercial shooting gloves are available, although an excellent shooting glove can be obtained by simply using an ordinary leather work glove or mitten.

Spotting Telescope. In most shooting events, a marking system or a spotting telescope is necessary to allow the shooter to see where his bullets are striking. The scope chosen should be light enough to permit easy carrying, but should have enough power and resolution to allow .22 caliber bullet holes to be seen at 100 yards, or .30 caliber holes to be seen at 200 and 300 yards. Twenty to twenty five power spotting scopes are best.

Spotting Scope Stand. A tripod or stand is needed to support the scope, so that the shooter can look through his scope to see bullet holes without moving out of position.

Cleaning Equipment. Consistent target accuracy simply cannot be maintained unless the barrel is cleaned thoroughly each time it is used. Many shooters will clean as often as every 20 shots during competitive and practice events. Necessary equipment includes a one-piece cleaning rod, several brass or bristle-bore brushes, bore cleaning solvent and patches.

The equipment listed here makes up the basic list of equipment every shooter will need to acquire in order to be able to participate in target events. Additional items of shooting equip-

Shooting ranges are built as elaborately in many countries as football stadiums and basketball arenas are built in the United States. This is an exterior, rear view of the range used for the Olympic shooting events in Mexico City, in 1964.

ment found in many shooter's gear include a kneeling roll, shooting mat, shooting glasses, cartridge block, rifle cases, equipment box or shooting stool, and various tools needed to adjust the rifle and equipment. The most important thing to remember, however, is that a lot of equipment is not necessary to get started in rifle shooting. In some events, such as metal silhouette shooting, for example, all that is needed is a rifle, some ammunition and a set of ear muffs.

The Shooting Positions

The first step in actually learning how to shoot in a target event is to learn how to get into a good shooting position. In the position shooting events, the first position that is learned is prone, the easiest and steadiest of the shooting positions. In air rifle or metal silhouette shooting, the only position used is standing. There, it is advisable to master the basic skills of firing a shot from a bench or rest position, and then to move into the standing position.

In getting into any shooting position, there is a sequence of steps to be followed in learning or developing the position. By following them closely, much time can be saved and mistakes avoided. The steps of this sequence are:

1. Study the position first. Learn how each of the parts of the body are placed in the position. Look at an actual position if possible, or use pictures and descriptions.
2. Get into position without the rifle. Try to put the body in the same position as an ideal position from the book or demonstration.
3. Get into position with the rifle and without the sling. Do not change the position of the body from the position developed without the rifle.
4. In prone, kneeling and sitting, put the sling on after the position has been developed without a sling. Do not move the left hand position from the previous step.
5. Begin by aiming at a blank wall—don't use a target. When the position has been worked out, place a target on the wall and orient the position on the target. Some sling and accessory adjustments may be necessary.

As each of the shooting positions is worked out, there are certain features to look for that are common to the best and steadiest shooting positions. The features to look for in good shooting positions are listed below:

Prone.

1. The body lies straight and almost directly behind the rifle. There is a 15- to 25-degree angle between the rifle and the spine.
2. The body is rolled slightly onto the left side. This is done by pointing the left heel up in the air and the right toe out to the side. The right knee may be bent and drawn forward.
3. The weight of the upper body and rifle is supported on both elbows, with 70 to 80 percent of the weight on the left elbow.
4. The left elbow is placed slightly to the left of a point directly below the rifle. Look for a straight line that can be

Russia's Valentine Kornev, World 300-meter champion in 1970, is shown shooting a 300-meter free rifle in standing position.

drawn from the left toe through the left side and straight out the left arm to the rifle.

5. The butt of the rifle is placed close to the neck. The rifle is held in position by the right hand on the pistol grip and the sling, which supports the rifle as it rests in the left hand. There should be no muscle tension in the left arm —the work of holding the rifle should be done by the sling.

6. The position of the head should be natural and comfortable. There should be no strain in the neck and no effort to move the eye forward to the sight.

Standing.

1. The feet are placed shoulder width apart, and are pointed 90 degrees away from the target.

2. The weight of the body and rifle is distributed evenly on both feet. The weight is shifted slightly forward onto the balls of the feet.

3. Both knees are straight.

4. The hips remain level and are not turned towards the target.

5. The shooter leans back away from the weight of the rifle and bends to the right and rear.

6. The left arm or elbow rests on the side or hip and acts as a brace to support the rifle. This arm is totally relaxed.

7. Choose a left-hand position that raises the rifle up to the height of the target without changing the back bend. The most common hand positions are to rest the rifle on the fist, or to support the rifle on the thumb and a V formed between the first and second or second and third fingers.

8. The right hand grips the pistol grip firmly. The right arm is held out horizontally, and pulls the rifle back into the shoulder.

9. The rifle is located so that only a slight forward tipping of the head is necessary to look through the sights.

Kneeling.

1. The shooter sits either on the right heel while the foot is supported by a kneeling roll placed under the instep, or on the inside of the right foot after the foot is turned and placed on the ground.

2. As much body weight as possible rests on the right foot.
3. The right knee is pointed at an angle of 40 to 60 degrees away from the target.
4. The back and shoulders are slumped down to keep the body weight low and to keep the back relaxed.
5. The left foot and knee are placed in front of the body and point to the target or just to the right of the target. The lower leg is perpendicular to the ground if the kneeling roll is used, or forms a 45-degree angle with the ground if the shooter sits on the side of the foot.
6. After the torso and body are slumped into position and relaxed, the left arm is extended forward, and the left elbow is allowed to rest on the knee wherever it falls. The torso is not moved forward to touch any certain or particular point on the knee.
7. The left arm supports the weight of the rifle with the aid of the sling. The left hand and sling swivel are moved back until the rifle is raised to target height.
8. The right arm is allowed to relax and drop down to the side. Light tension on the pistol grip is used.
9. The head tips forward only slightly as it contacts the cheekpiece to look through the sights.

Sitting.
1. The shooter sits on his buttocks and crosses his left ankle over his right ankle. Shooters with long legs and arms and proportionately short torsos pull the crossed legs back to form a cross-legged position. Shooters with proportionately longer torsos extend the crossed ankles out in front of them to form the cross-ankled position.
2. The body points 30 to 45 degrees away from the target.
3. In the cross-legged position, the elbows rest in the V's formed by the bent knees. In the cross-ankled position, the elbows rest on the legs in front of the knees.
4. The sling is placed high on the left arm, and the left hand and sling swivel are drawn back close to the trigger guard.
5. The left arm forms a natural straight line extension of the left side and shoulder. The left elbow does not go under the rifle.
6. The rifle is located high enough to permit a head position without excessive forward tipping.

The position is the foundation or platform upon which the act of shooting takes place. The purpose of that platform is to hold the rifle as steady as possible so that a well-aimed shot can be fired at the target. In developing that position, the shooter should first practice the position by aiming at a target and attempting to hold the sights as still as possible on the target. The shooter should learn to concentrate all his efforts on forcing the rifle to hold still on the aiming bull—nothing else in target shooting is more important than this effort to concentrate on holding the rifle steady.

Firing the Shot

Once the foundation of a good position is established, the shooter is ready to learn the basic techniques involved in firing a shot. No matter how steady the hold is, the rifle of even the best shooter is going to be moving slightly, and the actual firing of the shot must be done so that the shot is released when the sights are pointed at the ten ring. The act of firing the shot is actually a sequence of actions that takes place between the time the shooter begins to point his rifle at the target and when the shot is actually fired. These actions are:

Breathing. It is common knowledge that it is necessary to hold the breath while the shot is being fired. Most target shooters simply do this by breathing normally until the rifle is aligned on the target. At this point, a normal breath is taken, and after natural exhalation of that breath, the throat is closed and breathing stopped. In this condition, the lungs are relaxed, but still have plenty of residual air left to permit holding the breath for the eight to ten seconds necessary to fire the shot.

Aiming. Aiming is the act of aligning the sights on the target so that the shots will strike in the ten ring. Aiming involves: sight alignment, centering the front sight in the rear sight; sight picture, properly positioning the aiming bull in relation to the front sight; and sight adjustment, properly adjusting the sights so that the bullet strikes the target where the sights are aimed. The most common target front sight uses a ring or aperture, and the aiming bull is simply centered in the ring to form a series of concentric circles. The ring front sight must be large enough to show plenty of "white" around the bull. A post front sight is used in service rifle shooting, and in some other target rifles. With a post front sight, the bull should be held on top of the post, just as a ball would sit on top of a fence post. Target shooters prefer to see a fine line of white between the top of the post and the bottom of the bull. The proper sight picture for a telescope is much simpler. All that is necessary is to put the dot or crosshair in the center of the target or ten ring.

Arc of movement or hold area. No shooter has a perfect hold without movement. Even in a steady position like prone, there will be some movement while beginning shooters may have hold areas larger than the entire target. The shooter must learn to accept this arc of movement, and to center the hold area on the target. It is better to simply accept shots inside the area of movement than to try to fire perfect shots.

Hold Concentration. The most important thing for a shooter to concentrate on while the shot is actually being fired is the hold. Once the shooter begins to aim at the target and center his basic arc of movement, he consciously uses his mind to force his body to reduce the hold movements on the target as much as possible.

Trigger Control. As soon as the shooter centers the hold on his target and begins to concentrate on making the hold movement as small as possible, he begins another critical act in firing the shot, that of releasing the trigger. Champion shooters try to train themselves to automatically and subconsciously press the trigger when the hold becomes perfect. They teach themselves to do this by learning to squeeze or slowly press the trigger all the time a good hold is centered on the target. They learn to freeze this pressure and start over with a new hold if the arc of movement strays from the center of the target. They are not as concerned with exactly when the trigger is released as they are with getting a good smooth squeeze during the time when a small arc of movement is centered on the target.

Hold Timing. The best hold often occurs between four and ten seconds after the hold is started. The release of the shot should be timed to occur in that time period. If the shot is not released then, the shooter should stop, breathe and start a new hold.

Calling the Shot. Just at the instant when the trigger is released and the shot is fired, a careful mental note should be made of exactly where the sights were aligned. This precise mental picture or "call" is then translated into a location on the target where the shot should have gone, and is used by the shooter to determine whether the sights are properly adjusted, or whether some other mistake is being made.

Follow-through. There is a slight delay between when the trigger is released and when the shot actually leaves the barrel. Because of this delay, it is necessary for the shooter to concentrate on his hold until the shot actually leaves the barrel and the recoil has started.

Training

Once a shooter has learned how to get into a good shooting position, and how to properly fire a shot, he has learned the basic techniques involved in competitive rifle shooting. From then on, shooting means practicing or training in order to improve the shooting skills and reach the point where those skills will be good enough to do well in competition. For the shooter who has decided that he wants to get seriously involved in competitive shooting, there are several principles of training that should be remembered:

1. Set a goal. That goal can be anything from winning an Olympic gold medal to just having fun.
2. Plan the training activity. Work out a month-by-month and week-by-week schedule for reaching that goal.
3. Shooting improvement requires regularity and repetition. Frequent short periods of practice are more valuable than one or two long trips to the range each week.
4. Emphasize the most difficult positions. The amount and difficulty of training is determined by the goal of the training.
5. Keep complete records. Record keeping is used to analyze the performance and progress of the shooter.
6. Dry firing is often the most effective way to train. Use it in combination with range training.
7. Include competition in the training schedule. Learning to control match pressure can be done only in matches.
8. Good physical condition is important. The best exercises are aerobic exercises that increase heart and lung activity over relatively long periods of time.
9. Have fun too! Enjoying a sport is essential to having success in that sport. The shooter who enjoys practicing and shooting day after day is the shooter who will be able to practice enough to become a champion.

Getting involved in target rifle shooting means getting involved in one of the world's greatest sports. Many a competitive shooting enthusiast got his start by trying target shooting just to find out how good he was, and discovered that target shooting really means finding out how good you can become. That is the special challenge of competitive rifle shooting.

Concentration and Discipline

Steve Ferber

The precisely accurate delivery of a bullet to the target hinges on one requirement. If that requirement is met, all other factors having a bearing on the overall performance of the shooter—and the shot—will have also been in service at the time. These factors vary according to the particular shooting situation.

Perfect sight alignment is the requirement. Trigger control, hold, and follow-through are important factors. But the only critical time during a shot is the fraction of a second when the sear disengages to throw the firing pin against the primer, igniting the propellent, and thereby forming gasses which, under pressure, unseat the bullet from the case and send it through and out the barrel. We hear so much about the "lock time" of a particular rifle mechanism. The faster the lock time, the faster the bullet leaves the barrel when the sear is released from the trigger, and the less time for human error to develop.

If sight alignment is disturbed at that critical period when the sear disengages, etc., and while the bullet is still in the gun, you'll miss your target. If you're using a telescopic sight, and therefore don't have to consider aligning both a front and rear sight, but your sight picture is disrupted during that same critical period, you'll also miss your target.

"Aiming" takes a back seat in all rifle-shooting situations, save for the fraction of a second you use when you actually shoot. Too much importance is placed on aiming, when it's only a *promise* to do something. We all pick up a gun, throw its butt to our shoulders, and *aim* at some imaginary target—whether we're getting ready to do some plinking, or we're in a friend's den, or even hovering about at the sporting goods counter. And while we do that, we're looking at the barrel, or its sights, or the target—but in no way do we discipline ourselves during such an informal situation to concentrate on our sight alignment. Regarding aiming, we grew up with bad habits. To many of us, when we can see the front sight through the rear sight, and can also see the target, we figure we're "on." But we're not "on." Witness our imperfect shooting. Finding a target in and around your sights is aiming. It's easy and requires no skill. Concentrating on proper *attitude* of sights and target, and operating the trigger *according to that attitude,* requires skill, and is not easy. You need to discipline yourself and concentrate on the task to get off a good shot. And like everything else, it takes work.

Flinching disrupts sight alignment more than anything else, and it manifests itself in two basic ways—anticipation of recoil and jerking. Both cause the shooter to miss the target, and flinching is the main reason for inaccurate shooting among riflemen who are not entirely new to shooting. Even the best of shooters flinch more often than they'd like, and lots of factors can cause it. Obviously, if the shooter is afraid of his gun's "kick," or its noise, he's going to flinch, jerk and do everything else wrong. From that example, consider the refinements of the match shooter who operates machine-like in his precision and pattern. He doesn't really know when his shot will break, nor does he actually "hear" the report. He's not aware of recoil. He concentrates first on position, then sight alignment. He squeezes the trigger automatically when his sights are aligned and he has proper sight picture. But suddenly he's aware of the wind having picked up. Or he's felt a sudden chill. Or a cloud distracts him. At this point he's a flinch candidate—unless he works even harder to get back to the business at hand. It's easier for him to do that than it is for the average shooter because he's disciplined himself through practice. He knows how to concentrate on perfect sight alignment. When he misses his target—even ever so slightly—he'll usually know exactly why, and will be able to call his miss before he sees it in his spotting scope.

Once the skill of practicing good sight alignment is attained, skill at every other aspect of rifle shooting will be increased immeasurably. This includes both formal and informal target shooting, hitting a moving target—game or paper—and using both iron or telescopic sights.

Whenever possible, I teach shooters proper sight alignment with the *handgun*, even though the student's primary interest might be with the long gun, and for good reason. The short sight *radius* of a pistol (distance between front and rear sights) makes proper alignment considerably more critical than with a rifle (and its long radius). The truth is, if you can learn to shoot a handgun really well, you will automatically be a superb rifleman. Good riflemen are not necessarily good handgun shooters, however, and you don't *have* to be a good handgunner to become a superb rifleman.

The proof of this can be seen in the various military shooting teams. Though there are special problems with which rifle shooters must contend that are not shared by most pistol shooters—like doping wind—pistol shooters are often used on "pick-up" rifle teams, usually for long-range team events where a coach is "legal" during the actual slow-fire shooting sequences. At almost the instant before each shot, the coach will give the shooter final sight corrections—which constantly change—and the pistol shooter can be counted on to deliver. He's accustomed to critical sight alignment on his handgun. The long sight radius of a Garand M1 or an M16 is a pleasure to him. But he can't dope wind. And he'd be no good in the various timed- and rapid-fire rifle events either. But he knows how to hold and squeeze. Conversely, you can't put a rifle shooter on a pistol team, slow-fire event or not, and expect good results.

Why is *precise* sight alignment so critical? If you place two one-inch thick candles two feet apart and sit behind them and "align" them, you'll have no difficulty doing it. Now put a spot on the wall 15 or 20 feet away. Attempt to get a *sight picture* by aligning the candles and the target. Easy? Not so easy. You'll notice that the candles appear to be in alignment with the target, but you'll realize they're not *perfectly* aligned when you move your head slightly one way or the other. They'll come into better alignment when you concentrate more and move your head— and line of sight—ever so slightly. Doing it *precisely* will take a little effort.

Assume that the present set-up with the candles represents the short sight radius of a pistol. Now move the candles so they're six feet apart, representing the longer sight radius of a rifle. Align them with the spot on the wall. Immediately you'll see that it's not nearly as hard to do.

If the front sight of a pistol, having a sight radius of about five inches, is out of alignment with the rear sight by only 1/100th of an inch, the bullet's point of impact will be *three inches wide* of target at a distance of 50 yards! By contrast, the same mis-alignment with the longer sight radius of a rifle will not result in nearly as severe an error at point of impact. Furthermore, it's *easier* to get good alignment with a rifle—as I've already said. Easier, but not a shoe-in.

Rifle shooters using telescopic equipment don't need to worry about sight alignment, since the crosshairs, post or dot reticle is only one dimension, and the shooter needs only to put it on the target and shoot. However, extreme concentration is still required to do it properly because of a different set of problems.

When the shooter using iron sights concentrates on his sight alignment, he directs his concentration to the front sight, keeping it in perfect *focus*. Because the human eye cannot focus simultaneously on two points in different planes, the rear sight will always appear slightly out of focus when the front sight is in focus. Critical sight alignment is accomplished with the *front* sight. The target will be even more out of focus—a blur, really. If the front sight is blurred—because of focusing on the target— perfect sight alignment is more difficult to attain. With telescopic sights, the target is in full focus—as well as the reticle. But the target is also magnified. *Error* is magnified too. "Wobble area," which I'll explain shortly, takes on a different dimension with scope-sighted guns. Even though a new error factor is present using a scope (the reticle magnifying the fact that it's not where it should be), using the telescopic sight is still easier than the iron-sighted gun. But learn to shoot using front and rear sights. It's the best way to appreciate the importance of *preciseness*.

Go back a minute to what I said about point of impact error when front and rear sights are mis-aligned.

When you align your sights, and then form your sight picture (the target being the final point of reference) an imaginary line is drawn extending from your eye through the rear sight, to the front sight and on through to the target, touching all points. It's a perfectly straight line as it leaves your eye and finds the target, regardless of distance from the gun. But if the front sight is not placed in *exactly* the right attitude with the rear sight (perfectly in the center of the notch, having exactly the same amount of white space on either side of the rear notch, the top of the front blade exactly in line with both sides of the rear sight notch) you will miss your target. You'll miss by a fraction of an inch, or inches, or feet, or yards, or miles—depending on the distance the target is from the gun and the degree of mis-alignment. But understand this. The *front* sight may well have been in perfect attitude with the target at the time, which is why you were fooled into letting the shot break. However, its attitude with the rear sight was not perfect. There was certainly a straight line, it just didn't connect with all critical points—notch of rear sight, top of front sight and target—when it "left" your eye. The solution, then, is concentration. The concentration required to make that straight line extend from your eye through the three key points. Not to one side, above or below—but precisely through all three. Then you will have perfect sight alignment and perfect sight picture and will be in the perfect position for your shot.

Let's say your sight alignment is perfect but your sight picture is not. The front sight's attitude is not exactly on the target —deer heart, tin can, X-ring or whatever. You're holding two inches to one side of the target. The bullet will strike exactly there—only two inches away from your target, within your "wobble area."

When you're holding on a target with rifle or pistol, and unless you can lean it up against something, it's impossible to keep the gun perfectly still. The size of the wobble area varies with each shooter's skill, of course. It's really an imaginary circle around the target, which is small in the hands of a good shooter, and large when in the hands of a less-experienced shooter.

The important point is this. Providing your sight alignment is perfect, your target error will only be equal to your wobble error. If you're holding an inch off, you'll miss by only an inch. But target error due to *mis-alignment* of sights will be considerable, and will continue to increase in an extreme way as the distance between gun and target increases. Back to the scope sight for a moment. All the shooter has to contend with is wobble area —but it's magnified to the shooter according to the magnification of the scope, which tends to distress most unpracticed shooters.

If you're aligning your sights properly, you'll know if your trigger squeeze—or pull—is wrong, since if you haul back on the trigger improperly, you'll also throw off your sight alignment. You'll see it happen just before the shot breaks. "Dry firing," or pulling the trigger on a cocked and empty gun, is the best way to practice trigger control. The rules are easy.

Get into your shooting position—standing, sitting or prone —align your sights, form your sight picture and squeeze back on the trigger. If you see your front sight beginning to move out of perfect alignment—your squeeze is wrong. Many shooters use the pad of the index finger between the finger tip and the first joint for trigger squeeze. Others find the joint itself best. I don't know many good shooters who use the area between the first two joints for the squeezing area, but when a quick shot is needed in a hunting situation, I'm sure that area—and beyond—might come in handy. For practice, it's best to use one of the first two areas described. It allows for a *straight backward* movement that will not disrupt alignment. Pulling back on a trigger with the middle area of the index finger will result in delivering unequal pressure on the trigger, forcing it not only back, but also to one side. You'll see the results with your front sight. It will tend to move slightly to the right, or left, and out of alignment.

The only pressure you want to exert on the gun itself is also a straight backward pressure—into your shoulder, using your forearm grip to steady the rifle, or hold it up. Don't squeeze the pistol grip, just hold it hard enough to bring the buttstock firmly into your shoulder. If undue pressure is applied to either the forearm or the pistol grip, it will cause tremor—which, again, will disrupt sight alignment.

If you have all the time in the world, squeeze off your shot. When the time just isn't there for that, pull straight back—don't jerk the trigger back in an almost reflex action, or otherwise force off the shot. Gently *pull* back with even pressure until the shot breaks. Soon enough, when you've practiced dry firing and actual firing, you'll have the trigger control needed to deliver an accurate shot. It will take care of itself, as all aspects of rifle shooting will, once you've mastered sight alignment.

I've never believed in the existence of "the natural shot." We've heard many people accused of being such a shooter. But there's really no such thing. Good shooting is an acquired skill, and I also feel that the myth of the natural shot tends to work against other aspiring shooters. It's too easy for us to say: "Well, I can't shoot any better than I do because I haven't the 'natural talent' for it." It's true that some individuals have better reflexes than others, or eyesight, or tend to be less nervous than others. But the person who can shoot rifle, pistol and shotgun very well does so because he's learned a few things about shooting that applies to all shooting disciplines. He has the ability—or the will—to concentrate on each shot, and can apply his concentration to any target with any gun.

If you'll believe, for a minute, what I've been saying about the importance of sight alignment—that it counts most—consider it a step further. Look at the man who has taken shooting very seriously. He knew when he started shooting that if he leaned his gun against a fencepost, or on a similar rifle rest, he could keep his sights virtually free from movement, attain abso-

lutely perfect sight alignment and squeeze off a perfect shot . . .
each and every time. He also knew that if he didn't align his
sights perfectly at the time of the shot, he would miss his target.
Very early in his career, he learned his most important lesson.
And gradually, when he became more familiar with his gun, he
also became less distracted by its noise, recoil and so on. In
order for him to shoot it well *off* the rest, he had to practice.
When he practiced, he learned that he was only achieving something worthwhile when he put everything into it. When he wasn't
distracted by friends, for example, and wasn't preoccupied with
other thoughts, he worked at attaining the sight picture offhand
that he *knew* he could get by leaning the gun against a rest.
Something else was happening as well. He learned to "call" his
shots. More often than not, when a shot was bad, he knew why,
and more important, knew where it hit without seeing it hit. That
sort of thing generates confidence, and also the knowledge that
better concentration will guarantee better shooting.

A lot of things happen when such a shooter continues to improve. Because it is essential to *concentrate* on sight alignment
in order to achieve it, there's no room to think about other things
—like kick, or mothers-in-law—except fleetingly. And during
those periods, the gun is not shot.

Human beings can only concentrate on one thought at one
time. The genius, it has been explained, can concentrate completely on one subject for a period of only about eight seconds.
Most of us for five or six. What eventually happens is that the
shooter who learns to concentrate on each shot doesn't actually
hear it. He's tuned in to his sights, doesn't have to concentrate
too much on trigger control after a while (that becoming automatic) and understands completely why his bullet hits or misses.
And now he's a good shot.

So he's invited one day to the skeet field. His friends explain the different stations to him, he watches a few targets being
released and is handed a shotgun. But he has some special
knowledge too—even though he's never fired a shotgun before.
He knows all about *line of sight*, in this instance, eye to front
sight to target—and beyond target for lead. Since there's no rear
sight, he knows how important it is to sight as perfectly straight
down the barrel as possible, to the front bead, and beyond, and
worries about the fact that he can't get an exact sight alignment.
He's used to shooting a projectile no more than one-third of an
inch thick. The knowledge that his shot pattern represents a
"projectile" about three feet wide doesn't help him very much,

not when he can't truly "align" his sights, and he knows what mis-alignment will do. So what happens? He knows where his rear sight should be, and imagines its presence, forms his straight line, figures out the lead requirements by the second or third round of skeet, and starts to bust around 23 × 25 regularly. He also does something else. He moves over to the trap field, where he finds the shooters are more serious! And another "natural shot" is born.

About the Authors

Robert Elman has written a dozen books on shooting and the outdoors. He brings particular expertise to the historical perspective of hunting and the natural history of game animals in North America.

Bob Hagel was an outfitter and guide in Idaho before becoming an outdoor writer several years ago. Bob is a staff writer for *Rifle* and *Gun Digest*.

John Wootters, expert handloader, is Associate Shooting Editor of *Field & Stream* and is on the staff of *Rifle*.

Jac Weller is a frequent contributor to the technical gun publications and is a tireless researcher into firearm ballistics.

Russ Carpenter, a frequent contributor to the gun publications, is a gunsmith, and builds black-powder firearms.

David E. Petzal, Managing Editor of *Field & Stream,* is the author of several books and numerous magazine articles on rifle shooting.

Jerry Kenney is Outdoor Editor of the *New York Daily News*. He's an expert on whitetail deer hunting, and writes frequently about the subject.

John Jobson, Camping Editor of *Sports Afield,* has written hundreds of articles on big-game hunting many of which concern mule deer.

Bob Brister, an expert in all fields of gunning, is Shooting Editor of *Field & Stream* magazine and Outdoor Editor of the Houston *Chronicle*.

Jack O'Connor, author of several classic texts and magazine articles on guns and hunting, is Executive Editor of *Hunting* magazine.

Elgin T. Gates was the fifth man to win the Roy Weatherby Big Game Trophy. The number of his record-class big-game trophies exceeds 200.

Jim Carmichel is Shooting Editor of *Outdoor Life*. An extremely knowledgable firearms writer, he's the author of numerous magazine articles and shooting anthologies as well as the highly acclaimed *The Modern Rifle*.

Bert Popowski has wide experience as an outdoor writer. He's also an expert on varmint hunting, having written the classic book on crow shooting.

Gary L. Anderson is one of the best-known competition riflemen in the world. He's won two Olympic gold medals and holds six individual world records.

Index